Harmonic Trading: Volume One

Harmonic Trading: Volume One

Profiting from the Natural Order of the Financial Markets

Scott M. Carney

Vice President, Publisher: Tim Moore
Associate Publisher and Director of Marketing: Amy Neidlinger
Executive Editor: Jim Boyd
Editorial Assistant: Pamela Boland
Operations Manager: Gina Kanouse
Senior Marketing Manager: Julie Phifer
Publicity Manager: Laura Czaja
Assistant Marketing Manager: Megan Colvin
Cover Designer: Chuti Prasertsith
Managing Editor: Kristy Hart
Senior Project Editor: Lori Lyons
Copy Editor: Geneil Breeze
Proofreader: Water Crest Publishing
Indexer: Cheryl Lenser
Senior Compositor: Gloria Schurick
Manufacturing Buyer: Dan Uhrig

Pearson Education, Inc.
Publishing as FT Press
Upper Saddle River, New Jersey 07458

This book is sold with the understanding that neither the author nor the publisher is engaged in rendering legal, accounting, or other professional services or advice by publishing this book. Each individual situation is unique. Thus, if legal or financial advice or other expert assistance is required in a specific situation, the services of a competent professional should be sought to ensure that the situation has been evaluated carefully and appropriately. The author and the publisher disclaim any liability, loss, or risk resulting directly or indirectly, from the use or application of any of the contents of this book.

FT Press offers excellent discounts on this book when ordered in quantity for bulk purchases or special sales. For more information, please contact U.S. Corporate and Government Sales, 1-800-382-3419, corpsales@pearsontechgroup.com. For sales outside the U.S., please contact International Sales at international@pearson.com.

Company and product names mentioned herein are the trademarks or registered trademarks of their respective owners.

Printed in the United States of America

First Printing April 2010

ISBN-10: 0-13-705150-6
ISBN-13: 978-0-13-705150-2

Pearson Education LTD.
Pearson Education Australia PTY, Limited.
Pearson Education Singapore, Pte. Ltd.
Pearson Education North Asia, Ltd.
Pearson Education Canada, Ltd.
Pearson Educatión de Mexico, S.A. de C.V.
Pearson Education—Japan
Pearson Education Malaysia, Pte. Ltd.

Library of Congress Cataloging-in-Publication Data
Carney, Scott M., 1969-
  Harmonic trading / Scott M. Carney.
     v. cm.
  Contents: v. 1. Profiting from the natural order of the financial —
  ISBN-13: 978-0-13-705150-2 (v. 1 : pbk. : alk. paper)
  ISBN-10: 0-13-705150-6 (v. 1 : pbk.)
  1. Investment analysis. 2. Investments. 3. Portfolio management. I. Title.
  HG4529.C368 2010
  332.63'2042—dc22
                              2009051044

It is with the sincerest honor that I dedicate this book to my parents.
Without their never-ending love and support,
none of this would be possible.

Contents

Acknowledgments

I want to thank my family. They have been there for me through it all. I am truly grateful for their love, support, and encouragement.

My good friend and colleague, Jim Kane of KaneTrading.com, has been integral in the development of the Harmonic Trading techniques. He and I have collaborated on many strategies, and he has unselfishly provided tremendous insight to further this approach.

I would like to thank Mark Baker for his tremendous contribution to the Harmonic Trading methodology. Thanks, Mark. You facilitated this entire endeavor, making it possible for a multitude of traders to succeed.

I would like to thank Paul Desmond of Lowry's Reports for his encouragement, insight, and friendship. It means a great deal that someone of his caliber has taken the time to show an interest in new trading ideas and, more importantly, to know me as a person. Thank you, Paul.

I would like to thank Greg Morris of Stadion Capital. You are a remarkably accomplished individual who also has taken the time to show an interest in new market ideas and, more importantly, to know me as a person. Thank you, Greg.

Lawrence Roche of Battalion Capital has been a friend and a brother to me throughout the years. I don't think you realize how much I learned on all those trips to the Natural Gas pit at the New York Mercantile Exchange. These experiences and your incredibly positive attitude have made a tremendous difference in my own mental trading game and my life. There's always action. So let the games begin!

Gustave Calderon. Just thanks, G. As a friend and a brother and for everything, you have been there and reminded me of what is possible.

About the Author

Scott Carney, President and Founder of HarmonicTrader.com, has defined a system of price pattern recognition and Fibonacci measurement techniques that comprise the Harmonic Trading approach. He has named and defined harmonic patterns such as the Bat pattern, the ideal Gartley pattern, and the Crab pattern. He is the author of three books: *The Harmonic Trader* (1999), *Harmonic Trading of the Financial Markets: Volume One* (2004), and *Harmonic Trading of the Financial Markets: Volume Two* (2007). In 2005, Carney joined A.I.G. Financial Advisors as a Registered Investment Advisor. He has since left A.I.G. Financial Advisors after two years to start his own firm. In addition, Carney is a full member of the Market Technicians Association (www.mta.org) and the American Association of Professional Technical Analysts (www.aapta.us). He has been a regular columnist on several well-known websites, such as StockCharts.com, TradingMarkets.com, and eSignal.com. Carney is a featured guest on CNNfn, and he presents seminars nationally.

Introduction

Harmonic Trading: Volume One represents an important advancement of the gamut of technical trading strategies that seek to define opportunities in the financial markets through the identification of price patterns and the analysis of market structure. This analysis employs a foundation of several existing price-based measurement approaches to the markets, while adding many unprecedented strategies that create a synergistic system of rules to optimize the decision-making process of trading. Price pattern analysis provides precise and effective information regarding potential future trends. Most important, Harmonic Trading possesses unique and effective technical measurement strategies that define critical new patterns and expound upon the existing knowledge base of general Fibonacci and price pattern theories to establish precise guidelines and extremely effective predictive tools to define and analyze market trends.

As in any literary work, it is important to cite all appropriate references and original ideas that are discussed. I have researched extensively most of the relevant reference material that applies to the ideas covered in this book. I believe it is necessary to emphasize the preparation required to outline the Harmonic Trading concepts and the lengths that I have pursued to distinguish the origins of these ideas. Technical methods from Elliott, Gann, Hurst, Gartley, and others have been thoroughly cited as the foundation for many of the advanced concepts within the Harmonic Trading approach. However, it is important to note that most of these measurement techniques and analytical assumptions have not been presented previously. Therefore, the Harmonic Trading methodology may challenge previous technical theories and prove to be controversial. The ends do justify the means, as the strategies that comprise Harmonic Trading represent time-proven ideas that have served as reliable analytical guidelines in even the most volatile of market climates.

The Evolution of *The Harmonic Trader*

I want to thank the thousands of people who have bought my first book, *The Harmonic Trader*. It has been a rewarding experience for me to share this information. The response has been overwhelmingly positive, and I never could have imagined that it would have been so well received. I hope you find the material in this book as enriching and educational.

My first book, *The Harmonic Trader* (HarmonicTrader.com, L.L.C. Nevada; 1999), was a compilation of ideas based on several general technical approaches that incorporated new applications of existing analytical tools. *The Harmonic Trader* and the Harmonic Trading techniques evolved from a collection of individual strategies into an entire methodology to analyze price action in the financial markets over the course of many years. These techniques coalesced to define a unique system of rules for every step of the trading process. From the identification of a potential opportunity to exiting a trade, these techniques were designed to guide every decision from start to finish.

The Harmonic Trading approach offers pertinent technical information regarding the state of potential future price and specific levels of support and resistance. In fact, *The Harmonic Trader* distinguished itself from the outset by offering strategies that identified areas of potential support and resistance in ways that no other technical method had previously measured. The eventual evolution of years of experience culminated in the categorization of an entire system of pattern recognition of specific price structures based upon prescribed alignments of Fibonacci ratios.

The writing of *The Harmonic Trader* was a gradual evolution of many years of work that essentially arose from a great deal of trial and error. The book came together smoothly, however, as most of the initial work focused on precisely defining each of the basic patterns. Although the actual writing was no small task, the real work was organizing the file cabinets of charts, notes, trade journals, and the like into an effective and comprehensive "how-to" manual. In fact, most of the unprecedented ideas outlined in the book were the result of lessons learned from actual trades. I refined the strategies to devise a system of the most effective techniques to identify harmonic patterns. In doing so, several new strategies were presented that identified and defined new price patterns unlike ever before.

The system utilized new technical measures that proved consistently reliable and effective in determining potential future price action. In the development stages of this approach, I never stopped to question why such Fibonacci phenomenon was occurring. Rather, I continually strived to find the methods that were reliable and perfect the rules to define these situations. As the best relationships were identified, I classified distinct areas of specific price behavior that commonly developed in these specific situations. Essentially, I went with the techniques that worked! After compiling hundreds of charts and notes, I started to write *The Harmonic Trader*.

Initially, I compiled a list of Fibonacci strategies that repeated and the technical events that were consistently occurring within the framework of price patterns. Focusing on the peculiarity of exact combinations of Fibonacci pattern alignments, much of my initial work attempted to define the best situations among multitudes of possibilities. I realized early in my research into the best harmonic patterns that each setup was not the same. Although many potential pattern structures appeared to be similar, I realized that the alignment of points was a critical factor in differentiating potential trading opportunities and in providing vital information regarding the potential state of future price action.

After this discovery regarding price structures, I succeeded in defining the best alignments of Fibonacci measurements that validated each pattern. In the process, several unique concepts were outlined in *The Harmonic Trader* that shed new light on the measurement of price movements with respect to Fibonacci analysis. It is important to emphasize that **Harmonic Trading is different** from all other Fibonacci-related market approaches. Harmonic Trading techniques define potential trading opportunities with extensive precision and detail. Every price movement must be analyzed for possible information regarding the state of future price action. In addition, this approach utilizes unique rules and measurement techniques to generate valid trading signals.

As I have mentioned previously, others long before me have utilized Fibonacci ratios with price patterns. Robert Prechter and A. J. Frost in their book *Elliott Wave Principle* advanced the original writings of R. N. Elliott and clearly outlined Fibonacci applications with respect to their measurements of price movements. In fact, Elliott Wave analysis was probably the first comprehensive application of Fibonacci measurements to price pattern movements in the financial markets. Although Charles Dow utilized standard retracements (1/3, 2/3) in his tenets of Dow Theory long before Elliott, the aspect of relating Fibonacci measurements differentiates these methods and possesses greater technical implications beyond simple estimation. Regardless of the differences, various predecessors have applied similar tools and measurement techniques in previous literary efforts.

I would like to take a moment to discuss the material presented in *The Harmonic Trader*. The following list represents a few of the unprecedented ideas outlined in *The Harmonic Trader* that must be distinguished:

- **Potential Reversal Zone (PRZ).** Although many have discussed the use of simple Fibonacci measurements, *The Harmonic Trader* was the first comprehensive work that specifically outlined the concept of three or more Fibonacci calculations of a specific price structure converging at a defined price level as a potential zone for a change in trend. Essentially, the Potential Reversal Zone (PRZ) calculates resistance and support targets based upon the Harmonic Trading measurement techniques. In the years since this concept was introduced, it has been referred to groupings, clusters, Target Reversal Zone, and so on. Whatever the term, the concept was initially presented in *The Harmonic Trader*.

- **Distinguishing *all* points within the pattern.** *The Harmonic Trader* specified and differentiated every aspect of 5-point reversal structures by examining each Fibonacci point within the pattern, proving that not all patterns are the same. One of the most notable developments from this differentiation was the creation of the ideal Gartley pattern—a setup that required a 0.618 B point and a 0.786 D point retracement as the only valid alignment for the structure. After *The Harmonic Trader* was released, this alignment has become the industry standard for the structure.

- **The Mid-Point (B) as the defining element of 5-point price structures.** Another unique concept outlined in *The Harmonic Trader* was the significance of the mid-point (B) in 5-point price structures as the critical determining element for all harmonic patterns. For example, the B point distinguishes Bat patterns from Gartley structures.

- **Alignment of Fibonacci numbers defines the pattern structure.** After differentiating each of the patterns, *The Harmonic Trader* and Harmonic Trading techniques emphasized the importance of the alignment of Fibonacci ratios to differentiate each price structure. This discovery proves that similar structures are not the same. Furthermore, each alignment requires specific strategies that are common to each structure.
- **Alternate AB=CD pattern.** Among many of the unique technical measurements discussed in *The Harmonic Trader*, the Alternate AB=CD pattern was a vital advancement of the basic AB=CD theory, and it is a critical element within the Potential Reversal Zone of many harmonic structures.

In this book, the material reviews each of these concepts extensively and offers many new strategies to expand the arsenal of tools within the Harmonic Trading approach. It is important to note that the new ideas presented in this material build upon several existing technical approaches, such as Elliot Wave. These established technical principles are cited thoroughly to serve as a foundation for the numerous unprecedented strategies that are outlined in the Harmonic Trading approach. From this foundation, the techniques discussed in this book incorporate the best synergies of several Fibonacci-related strategies to define specific situations for potential trading opportunities.

HarmonicTrader.com

After the release of *The Harmonic Trader*, I launched HarmonicTrader.com. As the Internet became mainstream in the 1990s, I saw a website as a phenomenal opportunity to display the Harmonic Trading concepts as applied to real-time situations. Because most of the price measurement strategies were entirely new to the field of Technical Analysis, it was essential to define current market opportunities and maintain a consistently accurate record of predictive analysis. Therefore, the website was a vital forum to substantiate the unprecedented ideas outlined in *The Harmonic Trader*, and it was critical for me to prove that these methods worked—in any market.

At that time, the predominant bull market of the 1990s was about to turn and the Harmonic Trading concepts were about to be thoroughly tested. The website became an established track record that solidly reflected the ability of Harmonic Trading techniques to decipher price action in any market. For example, the monthly market reports consistently outlined numerous harmonic patterns that identified critical turning points in the major market indices. Specifically, distinct Bearish Gartley and Bullish Bat patterns in September 2000 and March 2003, respectively, were the defining harmonic patterns that pinpointed the critical turning points of the markets consistently for many years.

In the years that followed, the rally from the 2003 bear market low eventually led to yet more distinct long-term harmonic patterns that pinpointed another devastating market top. As difficult as the bear market of 2000–2003 seemed, the events of 2007–2008 financial markets were some of the most challenging conditions of the past 100 years. Through it all, the new measurement strategies enabled the Harmonic Trading approach to consistently define the most important technical levels in an unprecedented fashion.

In the past few years, the emergence of long-term bull markets in commodities such as energy, precious metals, and agricultural products shifted the trading focus away from nearly two decades of predominantly stocks to a more diverse palette of vehicles to consider. Not to mention, burgeoning currency market traders have fueled a new generation of online traders on an unprecedented international scale to expand the overall appeal of trading. Such diverse cross-market appeal has furthered the need for trading strategies to maintain a stringent unbiased perspective and analyze price behavior without favor. For these reasons, the Harmonic Trading approach has emerged as a reliable and effective system of rules to navigate any market.

Harmonic Trading: Volume Two

Since this book is titled *Harmonic Trading: **Volume One***, the obvious question is "Will there be a ***Volume Two***?" Yes, and relatively soon. *Volume Two* will contain advanced concepts that refine Harmonic Trading techniques to an extremely specialized degree.

It is important to note that *Volume One* is not a rehash of *The Harmonic Trader*. This book addresses several new patterns and trade management techniques that have not been discussed previously. *The Harmonic Trader* covered an extensive gamut of trade identification techniques. Admittedly, the other two aspects of Harmonic Trading, trade execution and trade management, were not sufficiently addressed. This material will cover the other two aspects of Harmonic Trading more extensively.

This book updates the foundation established in *The Harmonic Trader* and dramatically advances the application of the entire methodology. Several concepts, such as the Bat pattern, the 0.886 retracement, and the trade management rules, that have not been discussed outside my work on HarmonicTrader.com and other financial-related websites and organizations. However, several strategies, such as trend channel Fibonacci retracement trading and the Three Drives pattern, are important within the realm of this methodology but discussed only in *The Harmonic Trader*. This book advances the initial collection of strategies proposed in *The Harmonic Trader* and defines the primary principles of the Harmonic Trading approach.

Fibonacci and Harmonic Trading

The measurement strategies within the Harmonic Trading approach employ the somewhat controversial use of Fibonacci ratios. The recent popularity of the mystique of ancient codes has led to an unfortunate distortion of the true value that these methods inherently possess. In fact, it is almost hilarious that there are now numerous financial websites and publications claiming to possess the "Fibonacci Secrets," the Gann version of the Harmonic Trader, the quick Harmonic Trader, or the proper Fibonacci node levels that attempt to mimic the Harmonic Trading methodology. I say almost hilarious because most of it is not. The blatant borrowing of these techniques without proper citation and credit has become the standard in this industry,

I am sorry to say. In fact, most of the Fibonacci-related material on trading the markets is misleading and frequently cite only the well-chosen examples to demonstrate their techniques.

It is important to emphasize that Harmonic Trading is clearly different from other Fibonacci-related methods. Although others have utilized Fibonacci ratios to quantify various price patterns to identify potential trading opportunities, their application has been vague and not precise enough for actual trading situations. This was an initial frustration of mine when I first worked with these patterns, and it was a motivating factor to be as specific as possible in my analysis. Such specification led to the classification of *harmonic patterns* and even the defining of an entire analytical system that I coined as Harmonic Trading.

Essentially, I have been trading harmonic patterns longer than anyone. Period. End of story. How can I say this? Because there was not anything as specialized as the harmonic patterns until *The Harmonic Trader* was released. Furthermore, the other ideas presented on HarmonicTrader.com and other websites, such as StockCharts.com, eSignal, and others, furthered the basic concepts established in *The Harmonic Trader*. These unprecedented strategies have evolved into an entire methodology that I have termed *Harmonic Trading*.

Harmonic Trading is a sophisticated and comprehensive approach that utilizes specific and consecutive Fibonacci alignments unlike any other methodology. I am not trying to claim to invent the Fibonacci wheel. In addition, it is essential to me that all relevant original work be cited properly and thoroughly. From W. D. Gann to H. M. Gartley, I have credited all pertinent sources. However, Harmonic Trading utilizes many techniques and specific measurements that have not been presented previously in this manner. Furthermore, the strict approach of the interpretation of market price action from the perspective of harmonic price patterns is not the same as other Fibonacci-related Technical Analysis.

Although not exclusive in its analysis of price movements, these methods offer precise and accurate trading strategies that utilize unprecedented technical measures. From the 0.886 rertracement to the Bat and the Crab patterns, this approach is the most specialized and effective Fibonacci trading strategy. The Harmonic Trading methodology *is* a distinct perspective, and I assure you that "You will never look at the financial markets the same way again."

Chapter 1

Harmonic Trading

What Is Harmonic Trading?

Harmonic Trading is a methodology that utilizes the recognition of specific structures that possess distinct and consecutive Fibonacci ratio alignments that quantify and validate harmonic patterns. These patterns calculate the Fibonacci aspects of these price structures to identify highly probable reversal points in the financial markets. This methodology assumes that harmonic patterns or cycles, like many patterns and cycles in life, continually repeat. The key is to identify these patterns and to enter or to exit a position based upon a high degree of probability that the same historic price action will occur.

Harmonic Trading is based upon the principles that govern natural and universal growth cycles. In many of life's natural growth processes, Fibonacci numeric relationships govern the cyclical traits of development. This "natural progression" has been debated for centuries and has provided evidence that there is some order to life's processes. When applied to the financial markets, this relative analysis of Fibonacci measurements can define the extent of price action with respect to natural cyclical growth limits of trading behavior.

Trading behavior is defined by the extent of buying and selling and influenced by the fear or greed possessed by the market participants. Generally, price action moves in cycles that exhibit stages of growth and decline. From this perspective, the *collective entity* of all buyers and sellers in a particular market follow the same universal principles as other natural phenomena exhibiting cyclical growth behavior.

In an attempt to learn the origins of this analysis, many get lost in the need to understand why these relationships exist. The basic understanding required to grasp this theory should not move beyond the simple acceptance that natural growth phenomena can be quantified by relative Fibonacci ratio measurements. Applied to the financial markets, Fibonacci ratios can quantify specific situations where repeating growth cycles of buying and selling exist. It is the understanding of these types of growth cycle structures (patterns) that provides pertinent technical information regarding price action that no other approach offers.

The evidence of harmonic patterns in the financial markets can be found in price charts. A chart is nothing more than the collective record of buying and selling over time. Patterns that form over a particular period of time reflect a signal or technical "signpost" that can indicate the state of potential future price action. Furthermore, these situations have been historically proven to repeat and can identify significant potential trading opportunities with favorable risk-to-reward considerations.

After learning the basic requirements for each structure, it will take some time to develop the experience necessary to differentiate which price structures are valid trading opportunities. Although price structures can vary with respect to their Fibonacci alignments, Harmonic Trading techniques identify common elements of each situation that identify opportunities and maximize trading decisions.

Order within the Chaos

Many have argued that the financial markets are a random entity. According to the Random Walk Theory, popularized in the book *The Random Character of Stock Market Prices* by Paul H. Cootner (ed., MIT press, 1964), price action is "serially independent." This means that price history is not a reliable indicator of future price action. Although this theory does possess validity, since anything can happen in the financial markets, history has proven that within this randomness there is a degree of repetition.

Many events in the markets have repeated historically through the years. Significant corrections have occurred in October, which are usually preceded by a late summer peak. In addition, many common events such as defined levels of support and resistance or trend lines define repeating market action on a daily basis. Harmonic Trading techniques capitalize on such repeating market events by identifying specific price patterns within the randomness of the markets. Correctly identifying these situations is the key to profiting from these opportunities.

The identification of historically repetitive price patterns is the primary means that these techniques utilize to interpret the market's signals. It is in this effective price pattern identification ability that Harmonic Trading possesses its greatest advantages. The precision and accuracy of the specific pattern alignments define a consistent and effective approach that can be easily applied. Furthermore, each distinct pattern acts as a model for the basis of all trading decisions. Once a potential pattern is identified, the trading opportunity can be managed according to a defined set of rules that are particular for each situation. Although each pattern possesses different elements, Harmonic Trading identifies specific repetitive situations within the chaos of the financial markets.

Three Stages of Harmonic Trading

Harmonic Trading utilizes an enormous array of effective Fibonacci alignment combinations to define patterns. However, Harmonic Trading does not stop at the identification of valid patterns. Although it is the important first step in defining potential trading opportunities, specific rules and guidelines are required to maximize the management of a position. There is more to profiting from the patterns than just proper identification. The other aspects of trade execution and position management are equally as important to maximize profit potential and to reduce risk exposure:

1. **Trade Identification.** Regardless of what type of trading system is utilized, the initial step is identifying a potential opportunity. Harmonic Trading techniques utilize historically proven and repetitive price patterns that capitalize on overbought and oversold signals generated by the market's technical price action. A good portion of this material is dedicated to identifying and differentiating harmonic price patterns as quantified by Fibonacci ratio alignments. Understanding the differences among the various harmonic patterns is essential to capitalize on specific trading opportunities.

2. **Trade Execution.** After accurately identifying a potential trade opportunity, the actual trade must be determined. Several considerations must be assessed within a specific time period defined by the potential opportunity. The validity of the pattern must be determined, and the final action of executing of the trade or not must be considered.

3. **Trade Management.** After the execution action is decided, there are a variety of general considerations involved within the trading process. If the trade was executed, the position must be managed with specific rules to maximize the profit while minimizing the risk.

These three stages are important to consider as the general process of trading harmonic patterns. As I said earlier, any system utilized to trade the markets must identify a potential opportunity, execute the trade, and manage the position until it is closed.

If these concepts are new to you, I recommend that the identification of patterns be thoroughly understood before executing trades. The essence of Harmonic Trading is the ability to differentiate price structures based upon specific consecutive Fibonacci ratio alignments. Therefore, a thorough comprehension of the specific pattern price point alignments is an essential first step to successfully trade these situations. The other skills of effective trade execution and acute trade management are equally as important and represent the necessary elements to consistently profit from the Harmonic Trading approach.

Harmonic Trading utilizes the best strategies of Fibonacci and pattern recognition techniques to identify, execute, and manage trade opportunities. These techniques are extremely precise and comprise a system that requires specific conditions to be met before any trade is executed. The Harmonic Trading approach offers information regarding the potential state of future price action like no other technical methods. The unique measurements and price point alignment requirements are some of the unprecedented methods that differentiate this approach from other technical perspectives.

If you are new to Harmonic Trading, these techniques will open your eyes to many effective strategies that can indicate the potential future price action. If you have experience with these strategies, the material in this book will enhance your understanding of specific situations and offer many pattern-specific techniques that will improve your trading performance.

Chapter 2

Fibonacci Numbers

Origin of the Fibonacci Sequence

Fibonacci numbers are based upon the Fibonacci sequence discovered by Leonardo de Fibonacci de Pisa (b. 1170–d. 1240). His most famous work, the *Liber Abaci* (Book of the Abacus), was one of the earliest Latin accounts of the Hindu-Arabic number system. In this work, he developed the Fibonacci number sequence, which is historically the earliest recursive series known to date. The series was devised as the solution to a problem about rabbits.

The mathematical problem:

If a newborn pair of rabbits requires one month to mature and at the end of the second month and every month thereafter reproduces itself, how many pairs will one have at the end of "n" months?

The answer is: u_n

This answer is based upon the equation: $u_n +1 = u_n + u_n -1$

Although this equation might seem complex, it is actually quite simple. The sequence of the Fibonacci numbers is as follows:

0, 1, 1, 2, 3, 5, 8, 13, 21, 34, 55, 89,144, 233, 377... ∞ (infinity)

Beginning with zero and adding one is the first calculation in the numeric series. The calculation takes the sum of the two numbers and adds it to the second number in the addition. The sequence requires a minimum of eight calculations.

(0+1=1)...(1+1=2)...(1+2=3)...(2+3=5)...(3+5=8)...

(5+8=13)...8+13=21)...13+21=34)...(21+34=55)...(34+55=89)

After the eighth sequence of calculations, there are constant mathematical ratio relationships that can be derived from the series. Starting with the sum of the eighth calculation (34) as the numerator and using the sum of the ninth equation (55) as the denominator, the result yields 0.618.

34/55 = 0.618181 ~ 0.618

Repeating the process, the next division of the ninth calculation (21+34=55) and the tenth calculation (34+55=89) equals 0.617978 or 0.618.

55/89 = 0.617978 ~ 0.618

In the inverse calculation of these numbers, the same rules apply. After the eighth calculation, use this sum (34), but in this case as the denominator, and the sum of the ninth equation (55) as the numerator. This inverse calculation yields 1.618.

55/34 = 1.676471 ~ 1.618

Repeating the process, the next division of the tenth calculation (34+55=89) over the ninth calculation (21+34=55) equals 1.618182 or 1.618.

89/55 = 1.618182 ~ 1.618

These mathematical relationships remain constant throughout the entire Fibonacci series to infinity.

In the realm of Mathematics, the 1.618 is known as the *golden ratio* or Phi. The inverse (1/1.618) of Phi is 0.618, sometimes referred to as "little Phi." The 1.618 ratio is also commonly referred as the golden number or the golden mean. The number is denoted by the Greek letter Phi (φ). The inverse of the 1.618 (phi) sometimes is referred to as the golden ratio or golden proportion (0.618), and it is recognized by a small "p."

The Golden Section

A simple line can illustrate the relationships of the golden ratio or golden mean in the *golden section*. Begin with drawing a line and then divide it into segments where the ratio of one part to the entire line is the same as the ratio of the smaller part to the larger. The example of the golden section is illustrated in the following table:

Whole Line A = 1 inch (_____)

Section B = 0.618 inches   (_____)

Section C = 0.382 inches   (___)

A – B = C + B = A

|-----------------|--------------|---------------|-----------|

1 - 0.618 = 0.382 + 0.618 = 1

These line segments can be divided in various combinations to manifest phi (0.618) ratios.

- **Ratio of A to B = 1/0.618 = 1.618**

- **Ratio of A to C = 1/0.382 = 2.618 (1+1.618)**

- **Ratio of B to A = 0.618/1 = 0.618**

- **Ratio of B to C = 0.618/0.382 = 1.618**

- **Ratio of C to A = 0.618/1 = 0.618**

- **Ratio of C to B = 0.382/0.618 = 0.618**

The golden section is closely related to the golden ratio since the ratios have a relationship to one another that is equal to phi (0.618) or the inverse, Phi (1.618).

Ancient Examples

The 0.618 and the 1.618 constants from the series are found in the Great Pyramids. In addition, architects and artists have utilized the geometric proportions of the golden ratio in everything from the Parthenon of Athens to the works of Leonardo Da Vinci.

Examples in the Universe

In his development of the numeric sequence, Fibonacci was attempting to define the growth pattern of generations of rabbits as the example to explain particular mathematical relationships. Whether it's rabbits, elephants, or pigeons, the point to be understood is the mathematical sequence of growth patterns possesses Phi-related proportions that are exhibited throughout a variety of universal examples in nature.

It is important to note that both the ratios (1.618, 0.618) and the numbers in the sequence itself (...8,13, 21, 34, 55) are manifested in these examples. For example, the actual Fibonacci sequence of numbers can be found in the growth patterns of plants, whereas the golden number (1.618) can be found in the proportional growth of seashells. The human body possesses a variety of relative phi (0.618) ratio measurements, and even examples of planetary phenomena adhere to these golden proportions.

Fibonacci Phyllotaxis

Fibonacci Phyllotaxis is the discipline of studying and classifying the number of visible spirals, called parastichies, of flowers and seed growth patterns within plants. Most commonly, various plants grow seeds or leaves in patterns of successive elements exactly related to the Fibonacci sequence. A survey of plants of 650 species and 12,500 specimens displaying spiral or multiple phyllotaxis estimated that about 92% of them have Fibonacci Phyllotaxis. (R. V. Jean, Phyllotaxis: *A Systemic Study in Plant Morphogenesis* [Cambridge: Cambridge University Press, 1994]).

On many plants, the number of petals is a Fibonacci number. For example, buttercups have 5 petals, lilies have 3 petals, some delphiniums have 8, and daisies can be found with 34, 55, or even 89 petals. Fibonacci numbers can also be seen in the arrangement of seeds on flower heads. Sunflower seed heads, which grow in a defined outward series, typically possess either 34, 55, or 89 spirals. Cactus spines and pinecones show the same spirals as other seed head and leaf arrangements, but they are much more clearly visible.

Planetary Phenomenon

Not only do these constant numeric relationships occur in the Fibonacci series, there are also universal examples that exhibit this phenomenon. For example, Venus takes 225 days to complete a revolution around the sun. As we all know, the Earth requires 365 days to complete one revolution. If you divide 225 by 365, the result is approximately 0.618 of a year (225/365 = 0.616 ~ 0.618) and the inverse (365/225 = 1.622 ~ 1.618) results in 1.618 of a year.

Fibonacci Rectangles and Shell Spirals

Another illustration that exemplifies the Fibonacci numeric sequence starts with one small square of 1 inch on each side (see Figure 2.1). After drawing the first box, a second box of 1 inch in size is added in the progression of the Fibonacci sequence (0, 1, 1, 2, 3, 5).

Figure 2.1

On top of both of these, continue to draw 1-inch boxes, thereby completing a square the size of 2 (1+1=2). Again, repeat this process in the sequential order of the Fibonacci series, as a new square can be drawn that touches both a unit square and the latest square of side 2. This results in having sides 3 units long and another touching both the 2-square and the 3-square that now has sides of 5 units (see Figure 2.2).

Figure 2.2

In this sequential order, each square can be added with new squares having a side that is as long as the sum of the latest two squares' sides. Essentially, *Fibonacci Rectangles* are structures composed of squares with sides each a number from the Fibonacci sequence. From this succession of rectangles, a spiral is drawn in the squares, resulting in a quarter of a circle in each square. It is important to note that the spiral is not a perfect symmetrical formation since it is made up of a fragment of a circle. However, it is a good approximation of the kind of spiral formations that are manifested in nature and illustrates the relationships of phi quite clearly.

Utilizing the Fibonacci Rectangle progression, spirals can be drawn within these constraints that resemble the exact mathematical proportions of the shape of snail shells and seashells (see Figure 2.3). The spiral-in-the-squares begins with a line from the center of the spiral, increasing by a factor of the golden number in each square. So, each point on the spiral is 1.618 times as far from the center after a quarter-turn (per rectangle side).

Figure 2.3

Figure 2.4 shows a cross-section of a Nautilus seashell. The spiral curve of the shell and the internal chambers provide buoyancy in the water that the animal continues to grow throughout its development. Each chamber possesses defined relationships similar to the Fibonacci Rectangle example. In the same manner that the spiral was measured in the Fibonacci Rectangle, a particular line drawn from the center of the Nautilus out in any direction, locating two places where the shell crosses, will possess golden proportions.

Figure 2.4

The outer crossing point will be 1.618 times as far from the center, and the inverse resulting in 0.618, of course. This is one example in a variety of shells that manifest these phi relationships in nature.

Human Body

As the Nautilus shell example demonstrates, peculiar mathematical relationships are exhibited in many of nature's growth cycles. The human body demonstrates many of the same golden proportion relationships, as well. Each tooth is related to each other based on type. For example, the width of the central incisor is in the golden proportion to the width of the lateral incisor. The lateral incisor is in the same golden proportion to the canine, and the canine is in the golden proportion to the first premolar.

It is commonly known that the human hand possesses many golden proportions. Specifically, the individual bones in the index finger are related to each other by Phi. Starting with the tip of the finger to the base of the wrist, each section is larger than the preceding by approximately 1.618.

The human body manifests both the golden proportions and the numeric properties of the Fibonacci sequence itself. DNA molecules exhibit the elements of the golden section. Each molecule measures 34 angstroms long by 21 angstroms wide for each full cycle of its double helix spiral. The numbers, 21 and 34, are the seventh and eighth results of the Fibonacci sequence, respectively, and possess golden proportions.

From the unique mathematical properties of the Fibonacci series to the plethora of examples of this phenomenon repeating throughout nature, the most important concept to grasp is that there is some unexplainable universal order to many of life's cyclical processes. The realm of this discussion could fill an entire book. The mysteries of these golden relationships have been studied and debated for thousands of years. I believe it is important to understand the essence of this natural phenomenon, as such order in the universe has implications far beyond the financial markets. But, this discussion can be left for the theologian and the atheist to debate.

For trading purposes, these relationships, when applied to the financial markets, can effectively analyze similar cyclical growth patterns in price action quite effectively. However, it is important to not get caught up in the "why-type" questions that undermine the application of these methods. Rather, it is important to respect this phenomenon and master the discipline that such a perspective offers. As W. D. Gann proclaimed:

> *"I have always looked for causes and when once I determine a cause I can always be sure of the effect or future event which I predict. IT IS NOT MY AIM TO EXPLAIN THE CAUSE OF CYCLES."*

> (*The Tunnel Thru the Air* [Pomeroy, WA: Lambert-Gann Publishing, 1927], 78)

In this manner, it is important to focus on the application of the strategies that consistently work and not attempt to seek the deep philosophic justifications for their validation.

Harmonic Trading Ratios

Utilizing Phi (1.618) and its inverse (0.618) as the primary measurement basis, Harmonic Trading techniques identify price action that reacts to these defined levels of support or resistance. The gamut of Fibonacci numbers utilized in Harmonic Trading is either directly or indirectly derived from the primary ratios 0.618 and 1.618 from the Fibonacci sequence. The primary numbers, when utilized in combination with the *derived* ratios from the sequence, validate harmonic patterns and define the potential areas of change in price action.

It is important to note that some of the derived ratios are not entirely conceived from the Fibonacci sequence. For example, Pi (3.14) is more related through Ancient Geometry to Phi than directly calculated from the Fibonacci numeric sequence. But, Pi is effective in combination with the primary numbers 0.618 and 1.618 in the measurement of harmonic price action.

The ratios utilized in Harmonic Trading techniques are important as the primary means of differentiating price patterns and defining the state of potential price action. The essence lies within the specific combinations of these ratios that offer information regarding various price structures and identify trading opportunities. It is important to note that other technical methods utilize different percentage ratios. Dow Theory, for example, estimates general price movements by thirds (1/3 or 33%).

The primary numbers (0.618, 1.618) utilized in Harmonic Trading have been applied to Elliott Wave Theory for decades. Therefore, Harmonic Trading does utilize similar Fibonacci measurements as other technical methods. However, a variety of other derived numbers, such as the 0.886 and its inverse 1.13, are unique to Fibonacci trading methods. Although a few of these Fibonacci ratios have not been previously presented, others have utilized ratios like the 0.618 and the 1.618 in Technical Analysis for decades. Therefore, Harmonic Trading is not exclusive in this type of Fibonacci application to the financial markets. The true uniqueness and effectiveness of these numbers can be found in the combination of their specific ratio alignments.

This is the key difference of Harmonic Trading techniques versus other Fibonacci-related analysis. For example, many people utilize a simple 1.618 projection in their Fibonacci analysis. However, in certain situations, an 0.886 retracement can be a powerful level of support or resistance when combined with a 1.618 projection.

These relationships will be completely illustrated in the Pattern Identification section of this book. For now, it is important to understand that Harmonic Trading ratios are unique. The following list comprises the only ratios that are utilized to determine precise Harmonic patterns.

Harmonic Trading Ratios

Primary Ratios:

(Directly derived from the Fibonacci Number Sequence)

- 0.618 = Primary Ratio
- 1.618 = Primary Projection

Primary Derived Ratios:

- 0.786 = Square root of the 0.618 ($\sqrt{0.618}$)
- 0.886 = Fourth root of 0.618 or
  Square root of the 0.786 ($\sqrt{0.786}$)
- 1.13 = Fourth root of 1.618 or
  Square root of the 1.27 ($\sqrt{1.27}$)
- 1.27 = Square root of the 1.618 ($\sqrt{1.618}$)

Complementary Derived Ratios:

- 0.382 = (1-0.618) or 0.618^2
- 0.50 = 0.707^2
- 0.707 = Square root of 0.50 ($\sqrt{0.50}$)
- 1.41 = Square root of 2.0 ($\sqrt{2}$)
- 2.0 = (1+1)
- 2.24 = Square root of 5 ($\sqrt{5}$)
- 2.618 = 1.618^2
- 3.14 = Pi (See later section "The Importance of Pi (3.14) in Harmonic Trading")
- 3.618 = (1+2.618)

Primary Retracement: 0.618

Derived directly from the Fibonacci sequence, the primary 0.618 retracement is the defining element of many harmonic structures. In patterns like the ideal Gartley and the Crab, the 0.618 at the B point distinguishes these specific price structures.

Primary Bullish Retracement: 0.618

The primary bullish 0.618 (see Figure 2.5) ratio or retracement measurement is derived directly from the Fibonacci sequence. It is probably the best-known Fibonacci ratio. Although commonly and incorrectly referred to as a 2/3 retracement, the bullish 0.618 retracement is important support and frequently can be found in well-established channels. In addition, long-term 0.618 retracements can identify critical levels of long-term support.

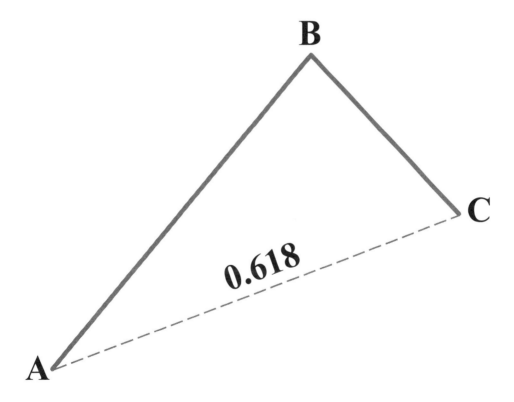

Figure 2.5

The bullish 0.618 retracement is often a defining Fibonacci number within many patterns like the Crab and the Gartley. In addition, ideal AB=CD patterns possess a 0.618 retracement.

Primary Bearish Retracement: 0.618

Again, the 0.618 is probably the best-known Fibonacci ratio. It is important to note that Elliott Wave measurements frequently utilize 0.618 retracements to project time and price targets. The bearish 0.618 retracement (see Figure 2.6) frequently can be found in well-established down-trend channels. In addition, long-term bearish 0.618 retracements can be critical levels of long-term resistance following.

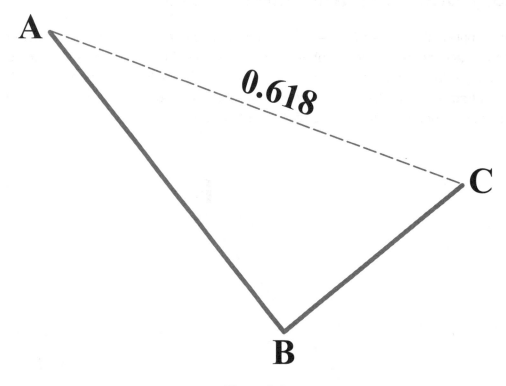

Figure 2.6

The 0.618 retracement—bearish or bullish—is most important in the Gartley pattern. Specifically, the B point of the Gartley must be at a 0.618 retracement. In fact, the ideal alignment for this pattern requires an almost exact 0.618 retracement to validate the pattern. In these situations, the 0.618 retracement can be very effective in differentiating harmonic patterns and identifying the best trading opportunities.

Primary Derived Bullish Retracements:
0.786 and 0.886

The Primary Derived Bullish Retracements of the 0.786 and the 0.886 (see Figure 2.7) are directly derived from the 0.618 ratio. The 0.786 is the square root of the 0.618. The 0.886 is the fourth root of the 0.618 or indirectly derived as the square root of the 0.786.

$$0.786 = \sqrt{0.618}$$
$$0.886 = \sqrt[4]{0.618} \quad \text{or} \quad \sqrt{0.786}$$

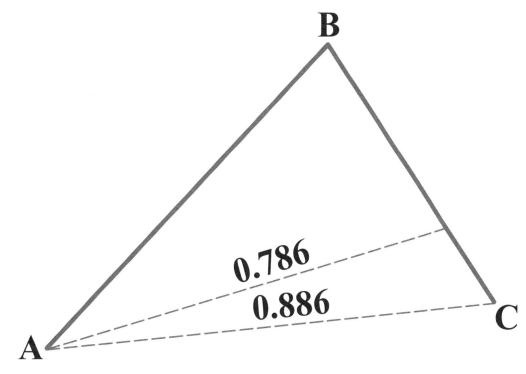

Figure 2.7

Out of these two simple Fibonacci retracements, I prefer the 0.886. I believe that the 0.786 retracement is more complementary in most pattern formations. Only in the ideal Gartley pattern is the 0.786 retracement a considerable harmonic number. The 0.886 is the most important retracement in the Bat pattern. In addition, the 0.886 is a critical number in the Deep Crab pattern, as the B point typically triggers 1.618 extensions. A bullish 0.886 retracement is usually an excellent entry technique to buy well-established support. Although the 0.786 retracement is more directly related to the 0.618, the 0.886 is a more critical number in harmonic patterns.

Primary Derived Bearish Retracements: 0.786 and 0.886

The 0.786 and 0.886 bearish retracements (see Figure 2.8) are commonly found in many corrective patterns. Again, the 0.886 is a more critical harmonic number in most patterns than the 0.786 retracement.

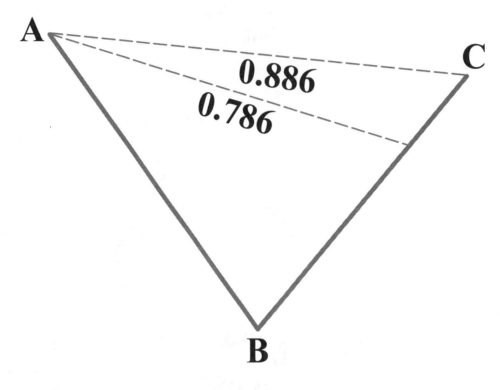

Figure 2.8

Although these two numbers are closely related in percentage terms to each other, their application in Harmonic Trading techniques can create vast differences in identifying potential patterns. In fact, the difference between 78.6% and 88.6% is more than a mere 10%. The 88.6% retracement differentiates the Bat pattern from the Gartley pattern. Although these patterns are similar in formation, their respective ratios define entirely different potential trading opportunities. This is just one example of the importance of being as precise as possible when analyzing harmonic price structures.

The Origin of the 0.886 Retracement

Although the 0.618 and the 0.786 retracement have been utilized in Fibonacci analysis for quite some time, the introduction of the 0.886 retracement is a relatively new discovery. Although I have introduced the ratio on various websites in recent years popularizing its use in the Fibonacci trading realm, I am not solely responsible for its invention. The 0.886 retracement was conceived through the collaborative effort of Jim Kane and myself.

Jim Kane of KaneTrading.com has investigated a gamut of Fibonacci-derived ratio levels for years. He and I have shared many ideas with each other that have advanced the field of Fibonacci analysis as it relates to the financial markets in an unprecedented fashion. In my opinion, the 0.886 retracement is one of the finest discoveries in Technical Analysis in the past ten years. The retracement is crucial in differentiating harmonic pattern structures and effective in areas of clear support and resistance.

Initially, I showed Jim a few different pattern structures in my attempt to prove that "not all Gartley patterns are the same!" Essentially, I was refining each 5-point price structure based on specific Fibonacci alignments. When it came to the 0.886, I noticed many specific commonalities that developed in price structures that accompanied the retracement. Specifically, I noticed that the B point within a Gartley-type structure that was less than a 0.618 would almost always exceed the expected 0.786 retracement of the XA leg at the projected completion point. I showed Jim this new pattern called "The Bat," which utilized a "deep 0.786 retracement." I told him that executing at the 0.786 without regard to the structure was a critical mistake. Besides, the 0.886 retracement when utilized in the correct pattern structures reduced the amount of risk in previously "undifferentiated" Gartley setups by 10%.

I showed him the relationships between the "deep 0.786 retracement" (0.886) and the 1.618 XA projection in the Deep Crab pattern. After we discussed the ideal Fibonacci alignments for the Bat versus the ideal Gartley pattern and in the Deep Crab, he said to me, "The deep 0.786 is really an 0.886 retracement, the fourth root of the 0.618 or the square root of the 0.786." Although I defined the price structures and specific Fibonacci alignments for harmonic patterns like the Bat, Crab, and Deep Crab patterns, I want to recognize Jim for his tremendous contribution to Harmonic Trading and recognize him for quantifying the 0.886 retracement.

Jim and I agree that it is the most effective Fibonacci ratio in the entire Harmonic Trading arsenal. In recent years, the 0.886 retracement has magically popped up on many trading-related websites. All I have to say is that if you see the 0.886 retracement on any website other than KaneTrading.com or HarmonicTrader.com, they are borrowing the technique. That's okay. But, it is critical to understand the nature of this Fibonacci level as more than just another retracement on the chart.

The 0.886 Fibonacci retracement is frequently the determining price level in areas of well-defined support and resistance. Valid reversals in patterns like the Bat frequently turn precisely at the 0.886 retracement within the Potential Reversal Zone (PRZ). Although these considerations will be covered later in this material, I must emphasize that the effectiveness of the 0.886 retracement, as an unprecedented discovery, is vital within the arsenal of Harmonic Trading techniques.

Secondary Bullish Retracements: 0.382, 0.50, and 0.707

$$0.382 = \sqrt{0.618}$$
$$0.50 = \sqrt{2.0}$$
$$0.707 = \sqrt{0.50}$$

The Secondary Bullish Retracements of the 0.382, the 0.50, and the 0.707 (see Figure 2.9) are indirectly derived from the Fibonacci sequence and the 0.618. These numbers are utilized only as complementary measurements within most harmonic price patterns. Therefore, trades are never executed from these numbers exclusively. However, these numbers are crucial in the differentiation of similar price structures. For example, the 0.382 and the 0.50 are commonly found as the B point utilized in the Bat and the Crab pattern. Although the 0.707 is less frequently utilized in Harmonic Trading ratios, it still complements "internal" Fibonacci calculations within patterns. The 0.707 is usually an intermediate retracement within a 5-point pattern structure. Again, the 0.382 and the 0.50 are more commonly found as definitive B point retracements in many patterns like the Bat and the Crab. In the Bat pattern, a 0.382 or a 0.50 retracement at the B point is mandatory for a valid price structure. Although the 0.50 is a more common retracement than the 0.382, these numbers are very effective in validating price structures as harmonic patterns.

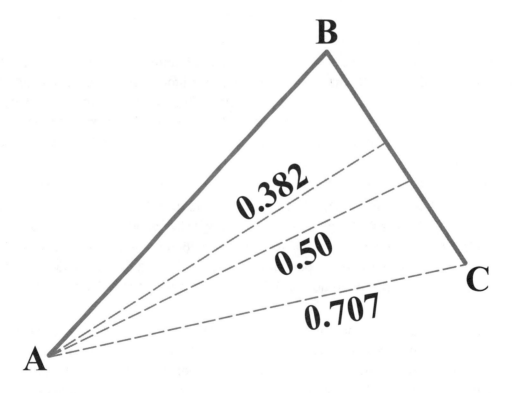

Figure 2.9

Secondary Derived Bearish Retracements: 0.382, 0.50, and 0.707

These secondary retracements are effective in defining certain patterns (see Figure 2.10). In addition, the 0.382 retracement is an important initial profit target following valid pattern reversals.

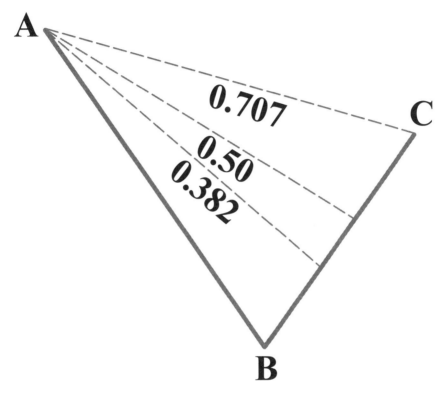

Figure 2.10

Primary Projection: 1.618

Derived directly from the Fibonacci sequence, the primary 1.618 projection is the defining element of many patterns. From a pure Fibonacci perspective, the 1.618 extension signals a state of extreme price action. As a general rule, this measurement frequently identifies the most critical area within a Potential Reversal Zone (PRZ). It is interesting to note that the 1.618 is utilized far more frequently as an entry point than its inverse, the 0.618. In fact, the 0.618 is mostly a complementary Fibonacci number, defining specific price structures as valid harmonic patterns.

Primary Bullish Projection: 1.618

The primary bullish 1.618 projection (see Figure 2.11) signifies an oversold state of price action. It is the defining measurement in the Crab and the Deep Crab patterns, and it is an important element in the Bat structure. In addition, the 1.618 extension works extremely well on intra-day time frames for short-term trading opportunities.

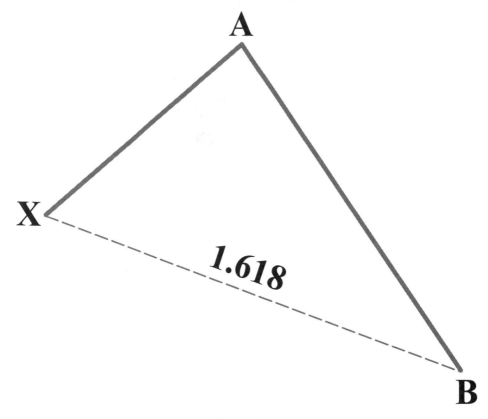

Figure 2.11

Primary Bearish Projection: 1.618

From a pure Fibonacci perspective, a 1.618 extension signifies an overbought state of price action, especially when other harmonic measurements exist that complement this resistance level (see Figure 2.12).

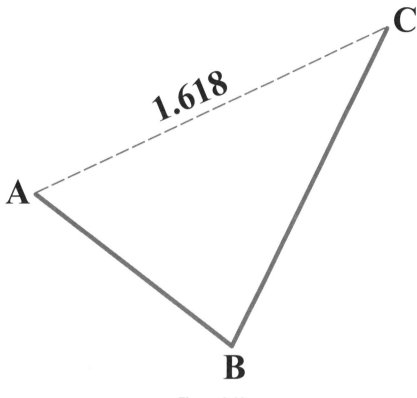

Figure 2.12

Again, the 1.618 extension commonly will be the most important number within a PRZ. The Crab and the Deep Crab possess critical 1.618 extensions that are the defining measurement within their pattern structures.

Primary Derived Bullish Projections: 1.13, 1.27

$$1.13 = \sqrt{1.27}$$

or

the inverse of the 0.886 (1 / 0.886)

$$1.27 = \sqrt{1.618}$$

The 1.27 is indirectly derived from the Fibonacci sequence via the square root of the 1.618 (see Figure 2.13). It is an important number in the *ideal* Butterfly pattern structure. The 1.27 BC projection is frequently found in *ideal* Gartley patterns, as well.

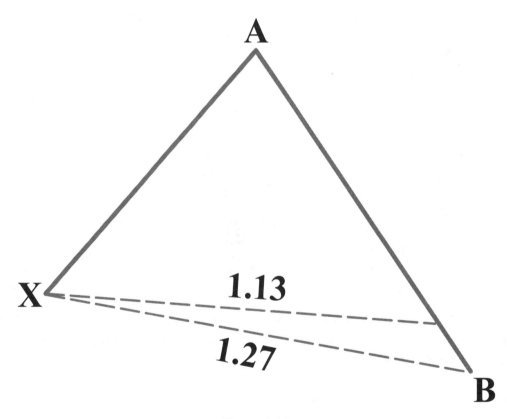

Figure 2.13

The 1.13 and the 1.27 are not nearly as important as the 1.618 extension. Although it is a frequent pivot point, the 1.27 projection must be utilized in specific situations. For example, the Butterfly pattern requires specific BC projections for the 1.27 XA price leg to be a valid entry point in a potential trade.

Primary Derived Bearish Projections: 1.13, 1.27

When combined with other specific Fibonacci measurements, the 1.27 can define precise harmonic zones of support and resistance (see Figure 2.14). Again, the 1.27 XA projection is the most significant number in the PRZ of the Butterfly pattern. The 1.27 AB=CD pattern is the most common alternate structure that is frequently found in the Butterfly, as well.

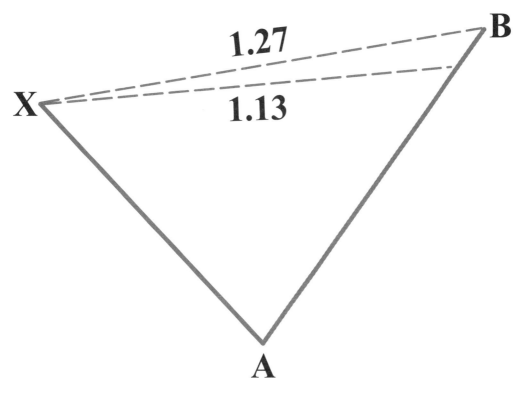

Figure 2.14

Secondary Derived Bullish Projections: 1.414, 2.0, and 2.24

The secondary bullish projections are most commonly found in BC measurements of patterns and merely complement the more significant numbers in a PRZ (see Figure 2.15).

1.41 = The inverse of the 0.707 (1/0.707)

2.0 = (1+1)

2.24 = The square root of 5 ($\sqrt{5}$)

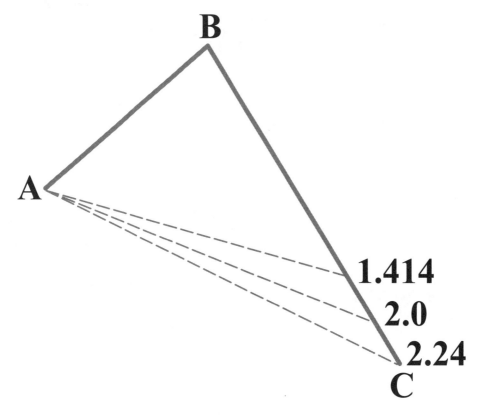

Figure 2.15

Although the 1.41 is less commonly utilized in harmonic patterns, it is as effective as the 2.0 and 2.24 when complementing other harmonic numbers at a pattern's completion point.

Secondary Derived Bearish Projections: 1.414, 2.0, and 2.24

Again, these Fibonacci measurements are extremely effective when they complement other more significant numbers in a PRZ (see Figure 2.16).

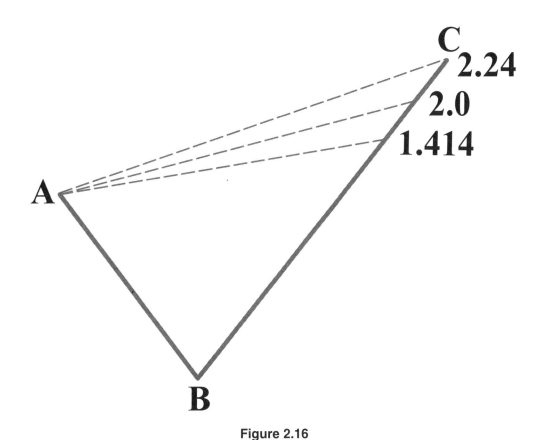

Figure 2.16

The 1.414 is commonly found in the Gartley and AB=CD patterns. The 2.0 and 2.24 usually complement more extreme projections in Bat, Butterfly, and Crab patterns. Some AB=CD patterns utilize the 2.0 and 2.24, but these are typically associated with extreme price action.

Secondary Derived Bullish Projections (Extreme Numbers): 2.618, 3.14, and 3.618

The extreme numbers are unique Fibonacci measurements. These projections are frequently found in Crab and Deep Crab patterns, as BC projections (see Figure 2.17).

$$2.618 = 1.618^2$$
$$3.14 = Pi \text{ (Explanation to follow)}$$
$$3.618 = (1+2.618)$$

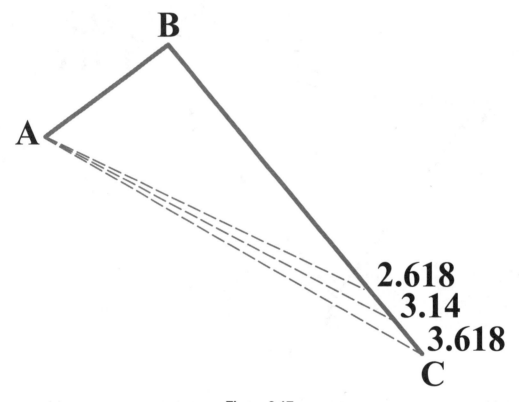

Figure 2.17

Although the 2.618 is clearly derived from the Fibonacci sequence, the 3.14 and 3.618 originated indirectly from the other Harmonic Trading ratios. The 3.14 (Pi) projection is a powerful harmonic measurement. The 3.618 is merely a complementary number in most pattern structures. In fact, the 3.14 and the 3.618 are mostly utilized as the BC projection in the Crab and Deep Crab patterns.

Secondary Derived Bearish Projections (Extreme Numbers): 2.618, 3.14, and 3.618

These numbers are usually found in patterns possessing extreme price action, hence the name (see Figure 2.18).

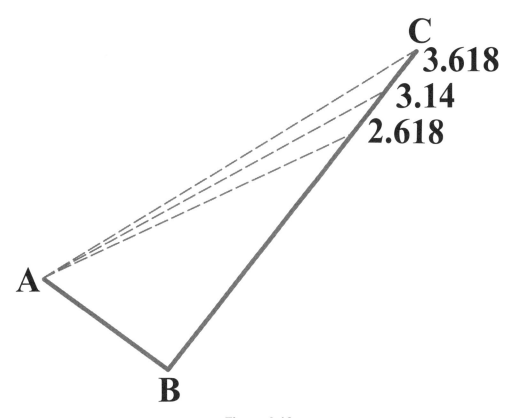

Figure 2.18

The Importance of Pi (3.14) in Harmonic Trading

Pi, which is denoted by the Greek letter (π), is one of the most famous ratios in mathematics, and is one of the most ancient numbers known to humanity. Pi is approximately 3.14 and represents the constant ratio of the circumference to the diameter of a circle. Known as the decimal expansion of Pi, it is impossible to calculate the ratio to an exact decimal place. Furthermore, no apparent pattern emerges in the succession of digits:

3.1415926535897932384626433832795028841971693993..... ∞ (infinity)

Like the Golden proportions, Pi is manifested in many of life's natural processes. The planetary bodies possess distinct Pi proportions, as well as the double helix spiral of DNA.

The importance of all Harmonic Trading ratios is that they are manifested in many of life's natural processes. The principles of Harmonic Trading are instilled in the origins of natural laws that govern many of life's cyclical growth processes. When applied to the financial markets, these measurements offer an effective means to assess the state of price action. Furthermore, these ratios serve as the primary basis that validates price structures as harmonic patterns.

Although these examples are present throughout the universe, it is important to note that Harmonic Trading is *not* Astrology. In recent years, certain astrological financial analysts and software programs have tried to align their approach with Harmonic Trading or, as it is also known, Harmonic Analysis. I believe people sometimes confuse the inherent natural aspects of Fibonacci relationships in Harmonic Trading to planetary alignments. Although these subjects may seem similar, they are not related to each other.

Harmonic Trading demystifies the frequently misappropriated use of Fibonacci analysis with respect to the financial markets. With the exception of Elliott Wave Theory, I believe Fibonacci ratios have not been clearly presented in recent years, and they have been frequently exploited as mere marketing tools for certain individuals. I am confident that this book will clarify the confusion of Fibonacci methods and provide an effective approach to define trading opportunities based on the specific application of Harmonic Trading techniques.

Chapter 3

Pattern Identification

What Is a Harmonic Pattern?

Harmonic patterns are defined by specific price structures quantified by Fibonacci calculations. Essentially, these patterns are price structures that contain combinations of *distinct and consecutive* Fibonacci retracements and projections. By calculating the various Fibonacci aspects of a specific price structure, harmonic patterns can indicate a specific area to examine for potential turning points in price action.

Specific Price Structures

Harmonic Trading techniques are similar to standard technical price patterns, such as the Head and Shoulders or wedge formations, since the focus on a particular shape of price action is the key validation factor. However, harmonic patterns are probably the most specific technical price patterns due to the specific Fibonacci measurements of each point within the structure. These measurements provide a tremendous advantage in that they serve to quantify and categorize similar price structures as distinct "technical entities." Depending upon the specific alignment of Fibonacci ratios within each structure, potential trading opportunities can be differentiated, offering pattern-specific strategies for each situation. In essence, similar price structures are *not* the same, and each pattern must be precisely defined. From such specification, a great deal of information can be garnered regarding the state of potential price action.

Elliott Wave Theory

The analysis of harmonic price structures is based upon the elements of simple Geometry and resembles the measuring techniques of Elliott Wave principles. I strongly recommend reading *Elliott Wave Principle*, by Robert Prechter and A. J. Frost. This profound work advanced the original writings of R. N. Elliott and offers a comprehensive explanation of the universal geometric relationships of natural law as they relate to price action in the financial markets. Furthermore, the Wave Theory and the discoveries of R. N. Elliott were some of the primary technical works that established the basic technical foundation for the identification of specific price structures based upon quantified wave counts.

Unlike the general structures of Elliott Wave Analysis, Harmonic Trading focuses on specific price movements. Harmonic Trading is unique in its approach of defining precise price structures, differentiating these movements with respect to their Fibonacci alignments. For example, most technicians are aware of the "M" and "W" corrective patterns explained within Elliott Wave Analysis. These corrective structures—either simple "abc" pullbacks or complex "abcde" formations—are vital in the validation of wave counts and Elliott Wave Theory. However, Harmonic Trading quantifies all of the Fibonacci aspects within a particular structure, further refining these "M's" and "W's" as unique technical patterns.

Harmonic Trading versus basic Elliott Wave Analysis:

- **The price point alignment of harmonic patterns is essential.**
- **Each pattern must possess an exact alignment that must not be violated.**
- **The most significant point in all harmonic patterns is the mid-point (B).**
- **Unlike Elliot Wave number counts, Harmonic Trading denotes each point with letters, marking each price move as XA, AB, BC, CD.**

Harmonic Trading analyzes and quantifies price structures with incredible precision. The specific rules required to validate price structures as exact harmonic patterns are unique and differentiate Harmonic Trading from all other technical methods. In fact, there is no variation permitted from the prescribed alignments of the harmonic patterns. This differs from Elliott Wave Theory, which allows greater variation within the realm of its price structure analysis.

There are many advantages in differentiating specific price structures. Such specification utilizes different strategies based upon each situation. Essentially, "all patterns are not the same." Although certain price structures may appear similar, the treatment of each situation depends upon the exact alignment of harmonic aspects that defines the pattern. This is one of the most important principles within the Harmonic Trading approach and is essential for turning patterns into profits.

W. D. Gann and Harmonic Trading

One of the most famous traders in history, W. D. Gann utilized trading methods based upon time and price analysis. Although many students of Gann's approach focus their attention on his application of geometric proportions based on the circle, square, and triangle, the true value of his work was revealed "in between the lines" of his many books, which emphasized the importance of respecting natural laws in financial market analysis. Although his methods are notoriously accurate—as evidenced by his performance in 1933 when he made 479 trades during the year, of which 422 were winners and 57 were losers—his profound writings offered a great deal of insight into the proper approach required to analyze the market. (Referenced from the W. D. Gann website: http://www.wdgann.com/pages/about_gann.php)

The premise of Gann's approach should be considered as one of the primary forerunners to Harmonic Trading. In fact, one of the earliest references to Harmonic Trading was mentioned in his 1927 book *The Tunnel Thru the Air* in which Gann stated:

> ***"But mathematical science, which is the only real science that the entire civilized world has agreed upon, furnishes unmistakable proof of history repeating itself and shows that the cycle theory, or <u>harmonic analysis,</u> is the only thing that we can rely upon to ascertain the future."***
>
> (T*he Tunnel Thru the Air* [Pomeroy, WA: Lambert-Gann Publishing, 1927], 77)

Although Gann's brand of harmonic analysis is more complex, including the use of his Natural Squares Calculator, both approaches utilize relative geometric price calculations of cyclical trends in an attempt to define critical turning points in the markets.

Fibonacci Pattern Alignments

Although many price structures may appear similar, they simply are not. The differentiation of patterns is the underlying basis and primary effectiveness of Harmonic Trading identification techniques. Like a combination to a safe, Harmonic Trading's precise Fibonacci price alignments unlock valid market signals in an unprecedented fashion.

In real trading situations, the specification of similar price structures that possess different Fibonacci alignments can substantially reduce overall risk. Furthermore, the ability to differentiate price structures is essential for identifying the best trade opportunities and handling each situation in the most effective manner. Differentiation is the key to successful Harmonic Trading, and it begins with the understanding that similar price structures are not the same.

This specification of Fibonacci alignments instills a disciplined approach that requires exact conditions to be satisfied before trade signals are generated. Although this can create situations where opportunities are missed if certain patterns do not reverse at the projected completion point, valid price structures become trade signals only when all conditions are satisfied. Such strict application of pattern identification techniques removes potentially dangerous and flawed strategies of flexible interpretations of price action.

One example that will be reviewed later in this book is the difference between a Bat pattern and an *ideal* Gartley pattern. Many people mistakenly believe that these are the same pattern. They simply are not. A Bat pattern is an entirely different combination of Fibonacci alignments than the *ideal* Gartley. In fact, I have seen e-mails and charting postings on the Internet over the past few years that frequently identify potential Gartley patterns, when the alignment clearly possesses a Bat structure. It is an example of strict application of different alignments like this that sets Harmonic Trading techniques apart from all other Fibonacci methods.

It is important to note that the strict application of any trading system is the primary basis for consistent performance—good or bad. Although this will be discussed in Chapter 11, "The Harmonic Trade Management System," the application of precise harmonic patterns offers a disciplined and consistent approach to trading.

Another essential principle of Harmonic Trading is founded in the belief that trading signals come from the market. Since Harmonic Trading utilizes quantifiable price patterns that have repeated historically, it is important to note that the price action is the determining element to define trading opportunities. After calculating the relative segments of each price structure, Harmonic Trading techniques quantify precise zones of potential support or resistance based upon their prescribed Fibonacci alignments. The price action must satisfy these conditions before any trading action can be taken. In this manner, it is the market that provides the signals required to take action.

The completion of patterns as market signals is based upon the notion that each segment within a particular structure can offer vital information regarding the potential state of future price action. The premise of Harmonic Trading's exact Fibonacci alignments that define specific patterns depends upon the relative measure of price action within each structure. This relative measure is known as the *Principle of Harmonicity*.

Principle of Harmonicity

J. M. Hurst outlined one of the most comprehensive references to Harmonic Trading in his *Cycles Course* from the early 1970s. His Principle of Harmonicity states:

> *"The periods of neighboring waves in price action tend to be related by a small whole number."*

(J. M. Hurst, J. M. Hurst Cycles Course [Greenville, S.C.: Traders Press, 1973])

The important concept to grasp is that price waves or distinct price moves are related to each other. Furthermore, Harmonic Trading techniques utilize Fibonacci numbers and price patterns to quantify these relationships, and provide a means to determine where the turning points will occur. From a general sense, the Principle of Harmonicity is the technical term that explains the basic premise of Harmonic Trading. The "neighboring waves" of price movements are utilized to identify and calculate potential trading opportunities. Harmonic Trading's focus on "neighboring waves of Fibonacci alignments" inherently grounds all trading decisions from a technical perspective based upon past and future price movements. Not to get into a long-winded discussion regarding fundamental information such as market news and other financial media-related stories that might affect the financial markets, the focus of all decisions within the realm of Harmonic Trading is dependent upon pure price action.

The strict reliance on pure price action to define trading decisions is essential to remain unbiased and open to all *technical* signals that are available. Relative measurements of "neighboring waves" do provide the necessary signals of potential market turning points. Harmonic Trading techniques determine market conditions and identify trading opportunities at price levels where the natural ebb and flow of buying and selling is changing based upon specific price patterns.

The precise rules that validate all harmonic patterns also create a system that bases all trading decisions on a defined *technical entity*. Specifically, trading decisions that are based upon individual patterns (the technical entity) fall within precise numeric ranges, where all elements, such as execution points, stop loss limits, and profit objectives, are defined relative to the structure.

This understanding that patterns create a "defined trading realm" promotes a sense of security, as all potential actions are defined in advance by the limits established by the setup and the price action behavior within this range. These concepts are easily understood with actual chart examples that will be covered later in this material. For now, it is important to understand that this approach generates valid trading signals based upon pure price action that is quantified by Fibonacci measurements and pattern recognition techniques.

Potential Reversal Zone (PRZ)

The concept of a Potential Reversal Zone (PRZ) was originally outlined in *The Harmonic Trader:*

> *"History has proven that a convergence of Fibonacci numbers and price patterns provides a highly probable area for a reversal.... This area of convergence is called the potential reversal zone. When three, four, or even five numbers come together within a specific area, you must respect the high probability for some type of reversal."*

(*The Harmonic Trader*, [Nevada: HarmonicTrader.com, L.L.C., 1999])

Specific price structures that possess three or more numbers within a defined area are the basis for defining these harmonic zones. It is called "Potential" because the defined area must be analyzed as the price action tests the projected "Reversal Zone." Although this concept will be covered extensively later in this material, it is imperative to understand that patterns are defined by specific price structures that contain combinations of distinct and consecutive Fibonacci retracements and projections. By calculating the various Fibonacci aspects of a specific price structure, harmonic patterns can indicate a specific area to examine for potential turning points in price action. Again, this area is called the Potential Reversal Zone (PRZ). In essence, a PRZ represents the critical areas where the flow of buying and selling is potentially changing. These harmonic zones attempt to identify the price levels where imbalanced overbought and oversold situations are reversing—at a minimum—back to their respective equilibrium level.

Any trading system attempts to be on the "right side" of the market—buying low and selling high. Harmonic Trading techniques quantify these areas and generate buy and sell signals based on the price action at these turning points. Furthermore, these techniques inherently define and direct trading behavior as a means of anticipating these potential changes in price action.

From a broader perspective, the identification of harmonic price patterns can offer tremendous technical insight of the state of price action. Past patterns and historically significant Fibonacci levels are an effective means of identifying important areas of support and resistance. Furthermore, each pattern provides additional information regarding the extent of overbought or oversold conditions in the markets that no other technical method offers.

The PRZ serves as a "harmonic window" that examines a specific price area with respect to the entire price structure. This concept places a great deal of emphasis on the price action within these windows of opportunity. Furthermore, the result of the price action in these zones is another defining element of Harmonic Trading.

From a general perspective, Harmonic Trading requires a *belief* that the markets provide the signals necessary to understand price action. Since all harmonic patterns represent the total sum of buying and selling relative to prior respective price action, each signal is generated from the market's own movements. In this manner, the relative analysis of past price action, as explained by the Principle of Harmonicity, is essential to define PRZs, to generate trading signals and to quantify specific structures.

It is important to emphasize that Harmonic Trading utilizes many unprecedented measurements to define critical areas of support and resistance. Exact alignments of Fibonacci ratios are the primary methods that validate price structures as harmonic patterns. In fact, the PRZ is truly a remarkable technical tool that no other method incorporates. Although these concepts will require some time to grasp and to integrate into your trading strategies, the Harmonic Trading techniques will always provide critical information regarding the state of future price action.

Chapter 4

The AB=CD Pattern

The AB=CD pattern is a 4-point price structure where the initial price segment is partially retraced and followed by an equidistant move from the completion of the pullback. This structure has been previously discussed in many technical works, and it represents the basic foundation for ALL harmonic patterns. The Fibonacci aspects in the pattern should occur at specific points. In the AB=CD, the C point will be a defining level for the completion of the pattern. Although the BC projection is critical in this structure, the most significant harmonic number is the exact completion point of the AB=CD.

AB=CD Reciprocal Ratios

In the AB=CD pattern, the alignment of Fibonacci ratios within the structure usually manifests specific reciprocal relationships. The reciprocal ratio of the C point retracement of the AB leg usually indicates which BC projection is utilized to define the Potential Reversal Zone (PRZ). For instance, a 0.618 retracement at the C point typically will possess a 1.618 BC projection that converges closest with the completion of the AB=CD. This reciprocal relationship within the equivalent AB=CD pattern defines the best PRZ for this structure. The reciprocal ratios that complement the AB=CD structure are as follows:

C Point Retracement	BC Projection
0.382	.24 or 2.618
0.50	2.0
0.618	1.618
0.707	1.41
0.786	1.27
0.886	1.13

The reciprocal ratios help define the completion of the pattern. However, the most important consideration to remember is that the BC projection should converge closely with the completion of the AB=CD.

The Bullish AB=CD Pattern

The Bullish AB=CD pattern is an excellent measure when looking at a well-defined sell-off. Although the symmetry may vary, this basic structure is a minimum requirement for all harmonic patterns (see Figure 4.1).

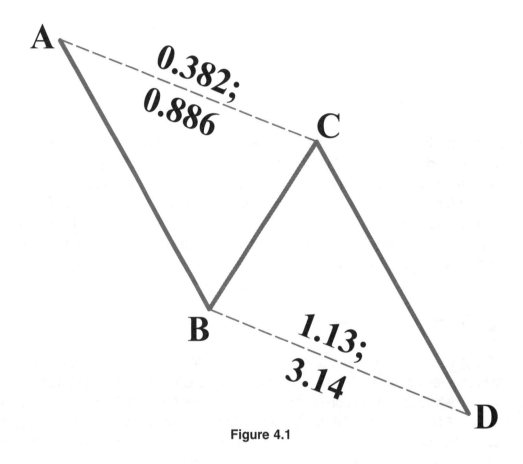

Figure 4.1

It is important to point out that the "0.382; 0.886" Fibonacci retracement range for the C point can be any of the Harmonic Trading ratios that fall between these two constraints. Therefore, the C point can be 0.382, 0.50, 0.618, 0.707, 0.786, or 0.886. Referring to the reciprocal ratios listed on the previous page, this correlates into a BC projection that can either be a 1.13, 1.27, 1.41, 1.618, 2.0, 2.24, or 2.618. In some rare cases, a 3.14 projection can be utilized.

Google (GOOG): Weekly

The first example of this weekly chart of Google (GOOG) shows a distinct Bullish AB=CD pattern with the completion point calculated at 267 (see Figure 4.2). The 1.618 BC projection complimented this area at 295. The pattern defined a Potential Reversal Zone (PRZ) of 30 points to buy the stock. Each price leg was approximately 300 points and required 6 months to complete.

Figure 4.2

The following chart of the price action in the PRZ shows an ideal reversal from this support level (see Figure 4.3). On the first week Google hit the numbers in the PRZ, the stock stabilized in the lower range of support. The stock held its ground and rallied nicely to reverse the downtrend. The following week, the upside breakout was confirmed.

Figure 4.3

This example illustrates an ideal reversal. When looking at a PRZ, it is important for the price action to turn in the area where the harmonic numbers define the situation. Clearly, this pattern identified a distinct support zone in the $265–290 area. The entire PRZ was tested and the price action reversed accordingly. Furthermore, the ability of Google to hold the low of the initial weekly test of the entire PRZ and rally above this projected support are excellent signs of a valid reversal at hand. This example is remarkable due to the precise symmetry and length of time that this pattern possessed. Each down leg required 6 months to complete and extended nearly 350 points. Although Google exceeded the exact completion point at 267, as the stock threatened to test the psychological 250 level, the price action stabilized the week following the complete test of the weekly PRZ.

When assessing the validity of a PRZ, it is important to examine the specific range to define where harmonic patterns complete. Although the exact completion of the Bullish AB=CD pattern completed lower than the 1.618 extension, both numbers defined the area under 300 to look to buy the stock. In these situations, the AB=CD completion point is the most important number of the pattern. In fact, the completion point of the AB=CD pattern should serve as a mandatory requirement before executing a trade. The 1.618 BC projection should complement the completion point area to validate the pattern. The key is to closely monitor the price action in the PRZ and look for the predominant downtrend to stabilize in the overall range defined by the PRZ. In the AB=CD pattern, trades will be executed close to the exact pattern completion point but the validity of the setup will be determined shortly after PRZ is tested.

Eurodollar (EUR_A0-FX): 60-Minute

Figure 4.4 is an example of the 60-minute chart of the Eurodollar (EUR_A0-FX) shows a distinct Bullish AB=CD pattern with the completion point calculated at 1.3426. The 1.27 BC projection complemented this area at 134.32. Again, it is important to consider the range defined by the PRZ. In this case, the AB=CD completion point at 1.3430 was the trigger for the setup. After selling off for nearly the prior three sessions, the Euro clearly stabilized before completing the reversal.

Figure 4.4

The following chart of the price action in the PRZ shows the reversal at the numbers in this harmonic support area (see Figure 4.5). After two tests of the PRZ, the price started to turn up.

Figure 4.5

Although the reversal required some consolidation to reverse the downtrend, the harmonic support identified critical support just under 1.3430. It is important to note that the ideal, exact AB=CD reversal are very obvious situations. However, the validity of any reversal depends upon the price action in the PRZ after all the numbers have been tested. Sometimes, a valid reversal is automatic. The price action hits the harmonic numbers and reverses nicely. In other instances, the situation may require some consolidation. Despite the time required, the focus should remain on the defined range in the PRZ after the numbers have been tested. In this manner, the PRZ creates a distinct window to examine and to assess the validity of the structural signal provided the pattern.

Dow Jones Industrial Average ($INDU): 5-Minute

Figure 4.6 shows an exact Bullish AB=CD pattern in the Dow Jones Industrial Average on this 5-minute chart. The Industrials formed this intra-day pattern with nearly identical time and exact price components. Each down leg was approximately 70 points. The AB leg required 8 price bars, while the CD leg entailed 7 price bars.

Figure 4.6

The completion point of the AB=CD pattern was calculated at 9306.75. The 2.0 BC projection complemented this area at 9312.21. The following chart of the price action in the PRZ shows the near-perfect reversal on the complete test of this support. After dropping more than 70 points early in the session, the $INDU hit the completion point of the pattern just above 9300 and started to stabilize.

Although the initial test nearly hit all the numbers in the PRZ, the third price bar was the clear trigger for the reversal. Figure 4.7 demonstrates the technical importance of the entire PRZ. The index stabilized on the initial test of this projected harmonic support before yielding a nice intra-day rally. The next several 5-minute price bars confirmed the reversal at hand, as the upside continuation indicated the strength of the pattern's completion point.

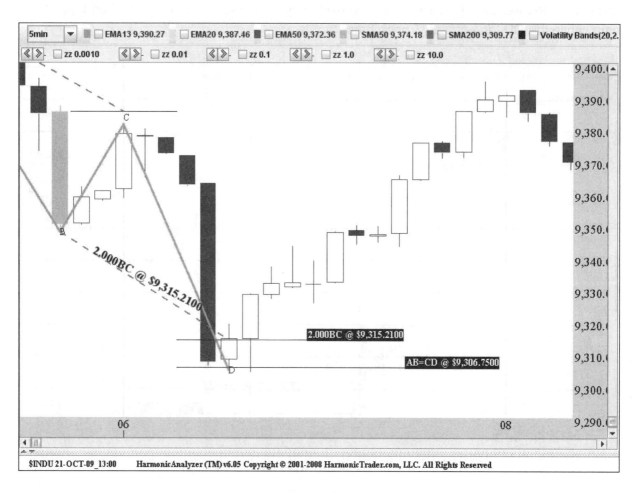

Figure 4.7

Another consideration is the sharp decline into the PRZ. Although the severe price action was a warning sign of a potential pattern failure, the ability of the index to stabilize immediately after hitting the PRZ is a strong factor in the validity of successful reversal. Not to mention, the reversal accelerated immediately after the AB=CD completion point was hit.

These are ideal signs of a valid reversal regardless of the timeframe. Although this was a 5-minute chart, the same principles apply for longer timeframes—60-minute, daily, weekly. The same technical principles should be assessed to determine the validity of a reversal from a PRZ.

NASDAQ Mini-Contract (Continuous)—(NQ_#F): 15-Minute

Figure 4.8 of the NASDAQ 100 Continuous Mini-contract exemplifies the ideal stabilization in the PRZ that valid patterns can demonstrate. The NQ possessed a considerable AB=CD pattern on this 15-minute chart. The BC projection converged in nearly the exact area as the completion point of the Bullish AB=CD. Both numbers defined the 1353 area as important intra-day support.

Figure 4.8

The PRZ in this example required several tests to validate the harmonic support. In these situations, the price action will require some consolidation to resolve the prior downtrend before reversing. Although this concept will be thoroughly discussed in Chapter 11, "The Harmonic Trade Management System," it is important to consider the time required for a valid reversal is typically relative to the size of the pattern. In this example, the price action stabilized as it tested all of the numbers in the PRZ. Despite the consolidation, the Bullish AB=CD pattern clearly identified the precise area for a long position.

Figure 4.9 shows the price action at the completion point of the pattern. Despite a somewhat severe decline into the PRZ, the 1.618 BC projection complemented the AB=CD at the 1353 level. The price action bottomed after testing all the numbers in the Bullish AB=CD Potential Reversal Zone. This situation provided ample opportunity to get long in this area, as the NQ reversed nicely from the completion of this pattern.

Figure 4.9

The Bearish AB=CD Pattern

The Bearish AB=CD should possess a distinct symmetry with the completion point of the pattern complementing the BC projection and defining a precise PRZ (see Figure 4.10).

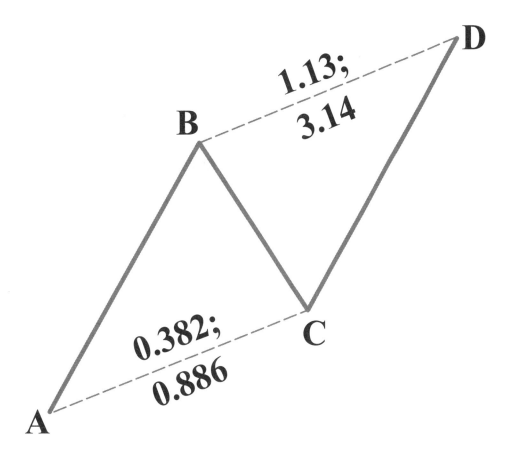

Figure 4.10

Again, it is important to point out that the "0.382;0.886" Fibonacci retracement range for the C point can be any of the Harmonic Trading ratios that fall between these two constraints. Therefore, the C point can be 0.382, 0.50, 0.618, 0.707, 0.786, or 0.886. Referring to the reciprocal ratios, this correlates into a BC projection that can either be a 1.13, 1.27, 1.41, 1.618, 2.0, 2.24, or 2.618. In some rare cases, a 3.14 projection can be utilized.

Goldman Sachs (GS): 15-Minute

This example of an intra-day chart of Goldman Sachs (GS) illustrates the ideal Bearish AB=CD structure (see Figure 4.11). The completion point of the pattern was calculated at 147.28 with the 1.41 BC projection complementing this area at 146.95.

Figure 4.11

These two numbers defined the 147 area as critical short-term resistance. It is important to note that the stock reversed after the AB=CD completion point was tested. Although the BC projection was an important calculation within the PRZ of the pattern, the completion of the equivalent AB=CD structure was the defining limit. The chart of the price action in the PRZ shows the near-perfect reversal just above the PRZ at 147.

The stock stalled after testing the entire PRZ and reversed several price bars later, as it stalled at the pattern's completion point (see Figure 4.12). This is another ideal reversal scenario. The price action in the PRZ clearly defined the do-or-die window of opportunity to short the stock.

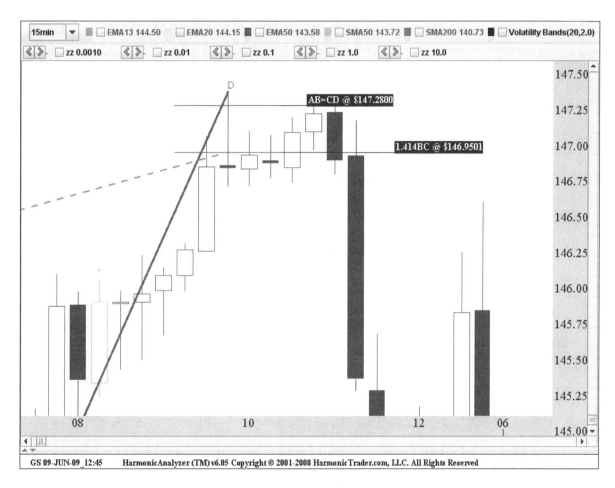

Figure 4.12

Although Harmonic Trading employs a variety of patterns to define potential reversal points, the same technical principles apply in the determination of price action in the PRZ. This case illustrates the ideal reversal situation and should be studied closely. In addition, the same principles apply, regardless of the timeframe. This example was a 15-minute intra-day chart. But, the same assessments of the price action stalling in the PRZ would relate if this was a 60-minute or weekly chart. The only difference is that the time considerations are obviously longer.

Philadelphia Gold and Silver Mining Index (^XAU): Daily

This daily chart in Figure 4.13 illustrates the effectiveness of distinct AB=CD patterns. Not to mention, harmonic patterns can be found in all markets—especially commodities. Gold can be extremely harmonic, as price action seems to respect Fibonacci levels more precisely than other markets.

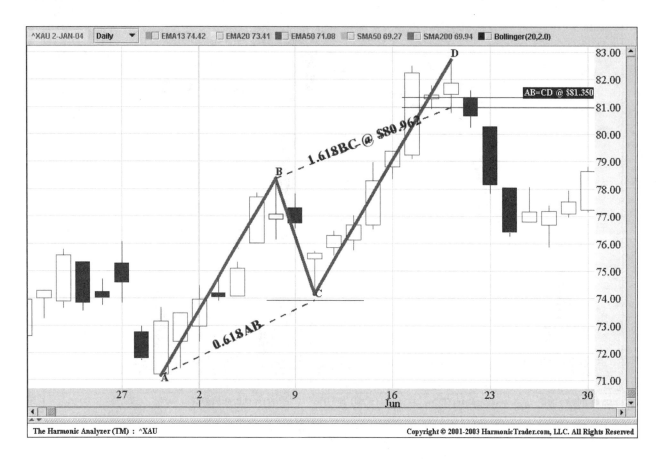

Figure 4.13

This daily chart exemplifies the elements and the effectiveness of Bearish AB=CD patterns. The XAU formed this pattern with the first leg (AB) requiring seven days, followed by a near-perfect 0.618 C point retracement and a CD leg that totaled eight days to complete. The PRZ in this situation was precise with the AB=CD completion point serving as the top limit of the range at 81.35. The XAU reversed 1 point above this level. Although this was not an exact reversal from the pattern completion point, the tight PRZ and distinct AB=CD structure with the perfect 0.618 and 1.618 ratios define this pattern.

Australian Dollar (AUD_A0-FX): 15-Minute

This example of the Australian Dollar (AUD_A0-FX) shows a distinct Bearish AB=CD pattern that defined an excellent short-term currency trade (see Figure 4.14). The completion point of the pattern was calculated at 0.9301 with the 1.27 BC projection complementing this area at 93.13.

Figure 4.14

The Aussie $ formed this pattern over the course of two full sessions where each up leg was approximately 100 pips. The setup clearly indicated initial short-term resistance just above the general 0.93 area. After rallying sharply up to the PRZ, the price action stalled at the numbers and showed signs of resistance. In fact, the price action failed to follow through to the upside after testing all of the numbers in the zone. Figure 4.15 shows the reversal after the price action tested the entire area.

Figure 4.15

This example possesses several interesting aspects that many valid reversals manifest. The pattern was clear and the completion point was well defined. The distinct change in the price action in the Potential Reversal Zone (PRZ) exemplified the impending change of the predominant trend. The stalling price action in the PRZ is typical of a valid reversal. In this case, the AUD possessed a tight range of numbers just above 0.93 to get short.

Standard and Poor's 500 September 2003 Mini-Contract (ES_U3): 60-Minute

A few years ago, I provided a daily advisory service. I would identify potential trades by outlining the various critical ratios and patterns that were near completion. The next examples are from these reports and reflect actual trading situations. These reports can be referenced on HarmonicTrader.com. Furthermore, these demonstrate a real-time application of this approach. These examples both show intra-day Bearish AB=CD patterns in the S&P 500 September 2003 Mini-contract (ES).

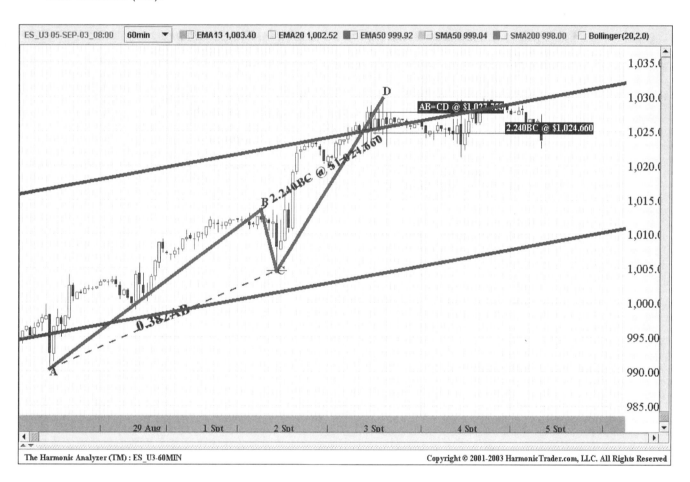

Figure 4.16

I trade the minis regularly and frequently utilize the AB=CD patterns as a means of defining intra-day pivot points. On this day, the ES formed an intra-day Bearish AB=CD pattern with the completion point at 1023.75 and the 2.24 BC projection at 1024.65. The next chart of the price action in the Potential Reversal Zone (PRZ) clearly shows the roll over at the completion point of the Bearish AB=CD at 1027.75.

For the daily commentary on the website, I posted a note before the market opened. Based upon the pattern at hand, I identified a distinct short-term trading opportunity in the Standard and Poor's 500 Index Mini-contract. On this particular morning, I was assessing the Bearish AB=CD pattern that identified a selling opportunity in this PRZ. Before the market opened on September 4th, I wrote:

"For today's immediate action, the ES is off 2 $\frac{1}{2}$. The ES will likely attempt to retest the Bearish AB=CD at 1028 and fill today's upside gap. This should offer an early shorting opportunity.

With the ES testing the top range of the bullish channel, I would look for the ES to correct this week's rally off this resistance for a move to test this Bullish AB=CD at 1020. This area is also prior harmonic resistance of this Bearish AB=CD at 1020 acting as support."

(HarmonicTrader.com, 09/04/03; http://www.HarmonicTrader.com/ members/harmonic/home/miniroom090403.htm)

The chart in Figure 4.17 of the price action in the PRZ shows the resistance experienced by the ES over the course of three days (September 3–5, 2003). The Bearish AB=CD pattern indicated the area to sell the ES, and the price action tested this resistance three times before the ultimate reversal. On the day of September 4, the ES rallied back to retest the Bearish AB=CD completion point at the 1028 level. By the following day, the ES hit the 1020 profit target outlined in the previous morning's report.

Figure 4.17

I realized that this Bearish AB=CD pattern was valid short-term resistance because of the initial action at the PRZ. The first test of the PRZ on the prior day held firm, as the 1028 area defined precise short-term resistance. Although a secondary retest of this PRZ was required, the pattern clearly defined the ideal area to sell.

It is important to note that multiple tests of a distinct PRZ are common, especially in short-term trading situations like these. Furthermore, multiple tests of harmonic patterns can serve to confirm support and resistance levels. This was the case with the ES.

The next 60-minute chart of the Standard and Poor's 500 September 2003 Mini-Contract (ES_U3) shows another distinct Bearish AB=CD that reversed sharply from the completion point of the pattern (see Figure 4.18).

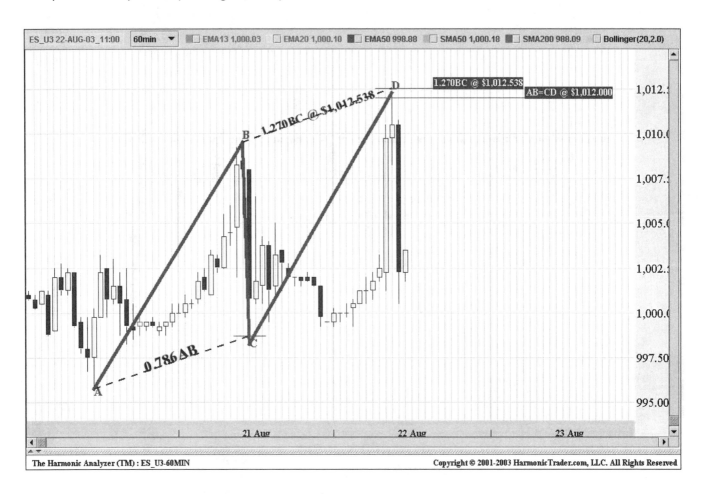

Figure 4.18

The chart in Figure 4.19 of the price action in the PRZ shows a precise reversal ¼ point above the completion of the pattern. Although the peak fell shy of the 1.27 BC projection at 1012.50, the pattern clearly indicated that the 1012 area was a selling opportunity.

A sharp reversal like this can be difficult to catch sometimes. This example demonstrates the precision that Bearish AB=CD patterns possess, especially on intra-day time intervals, although long-term situations can be as precise. The key is to identify the pattern's completion point and to execute trades in the PRZ. The most important aspect is to focus on the price action after the entire zone has been tested. A valid reversal should clearly begin to stall at the numbers and change the direction of the predominant trend.

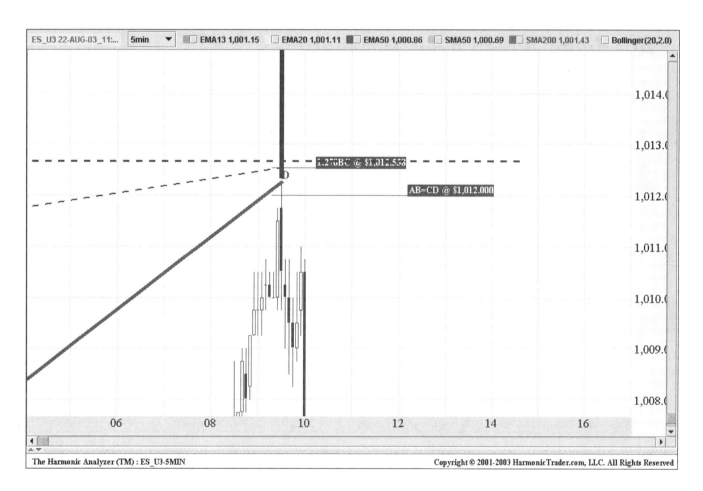

Figure 4.19

Alternate AB=CD Patterns

Since the AB=CD pattern is the basic framework of all harmonic patterns, it is an essential consideration in defining any Potential Reversal Zone (PRZ). Although the AB=CD equivalent patterns have been utilized by technicians for quite some time, the idea of an alternate calculation to define other harmonic patterns was originally outlined in *The Harmonic Trader*. Alternate patterns provide an effective means of complementing other significant Fibonacci calculations, especially when the equivalent AB=CD is not relevant for a particular setup. The Alternate AB=CD pattern differentiates similar structures, as well.

Alternate Bullish AB=CD Pattern

The Alternate Bullish AB=CD pattern (see Figure 4.20) typically develops in patterns like the Bullish Crab and the Bullish Butterfly in extended sell-offs. However, the Alternate AB=CD pattern is merely a complementary measure relative to other Fibonacci numbers in the PRZ. In addition, equivalent AB=CD patterns usually possess more significant completion points than the alternate structures. The 1.618 AB=CD pattern is utilized less frequently than the other AB=CD combinations. Despite the variations, each AB=CD measurement, when applied to correct the harmonic pattern can define precise reversal areas and offer an effective means to quantify price structures.

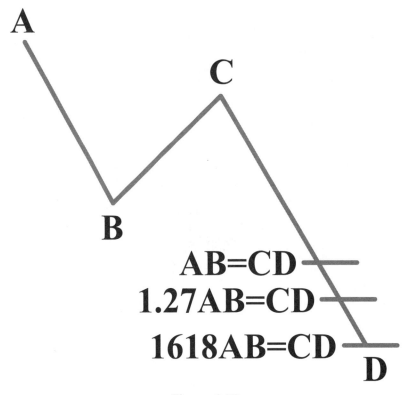

Figure 4.20

Alternate Bearish AB=CD Pattern

It is important to note that the AB=CD pattern—equivalent or alternate—is the basis for all harmonic structures (see Figure 4.21). In most setups, the equivalent AB=CD pattern is a minimum requirement before entering a trade. When combined with other significant Fibonacci retracements and projections, the AB=CD pattern can define excellent reversal areas.

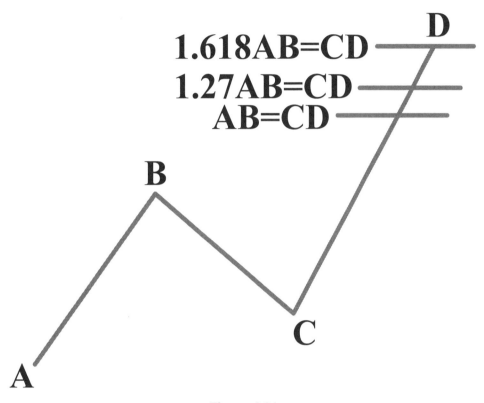

Figure 4.21

The alternate variations the AB=CD are frequently found in those patterns with an extended CD leg. Unlike a Gartley, which utilizes an equivalent AB=CD, the Bat structure typically experiences an Alternate 1.27 AB=CD pattern. These two similar patterns require completely different AB=CD conditions to validate their respective structures. However, this degree of differentiation increases the validity of pattern identification techniques and reduces the overall risk by defining the most precise PRZ.

The Perfect AB=CD Pattern

The Perfect AB=CD pattern is primarily defined by the C point that should be a precise 0.618 retracement of the AB leg. Ideally, the B point should be tested but not exceeded measurably. The 0.618 C point retracement sets up the 1.618 BC projection. Although a 1.618 extension usually indicates an extreme area from a Fibonacci perspective, these frequently yield significant reactions, especially in perfect AB=CD patterns.

These structures are typically quite symmetrical and possess the most ideal of geometric structures. For obvious reasons, the 0.618 and 1.618 within the perfect AB=CD pattern represent the most harmonic ratios that are directly derived from the Fibonacci sequence. Another aspect of the perfect AB=CD pattern is the general time consideration, where each leg should be exactly equivalent in duration. Although an exact time length for each price leg is not required, each segment of the pattern should be distinctly symmetrical.

1. **Precise 0.618 C point retracement of the AB leg**
2. **1.618 BC projection**
3. **Equivalent time duration for each leg**

The Perfect Bullish AB=CD Pattern

The perfect Bullish AB=CD pattern is usually a distinct structure that adheres to a precise symmetry and mandatory Fibonacci pivot points (see Figure 4.22). The AB=CD completion point should be the lowest number in the PRZ and converge in the same area with the 1.618 BC projection.

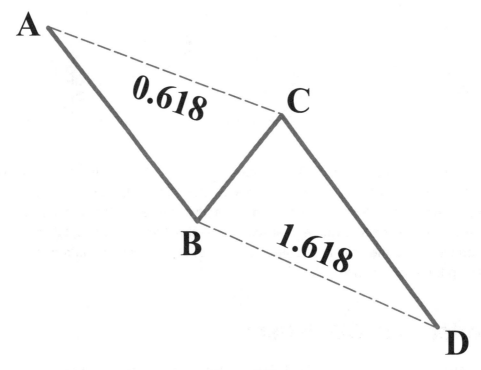

Figure 4.22

NASDAQ 100 March 2004 Mini-Contract (NQ_H4): 10-Minute

The chart in Figure 4.23 is a clear example of a perfect Bullish AB=CD pattern with the completion point calculated and the 1.618 BC projection converging within a tight range. In addition, the symmetry of the pattern is distinct. In this case, each down leg (AB, CD) was six 10-minute bars. It is important to note that the AB=CD completion point at 1379 was the defining limit in the PRZ. In a perfect Bullish AB=CD, the completion point of the AB=CD should sit below the 1.618 XA projection.

Figure 4.23

The Perfect Bearish AB=CD Pattern

The perfect Bearish AB=CD pattern is a distinct structure that adheres to precise Fibonacci pivot points (see Figure 4.24).

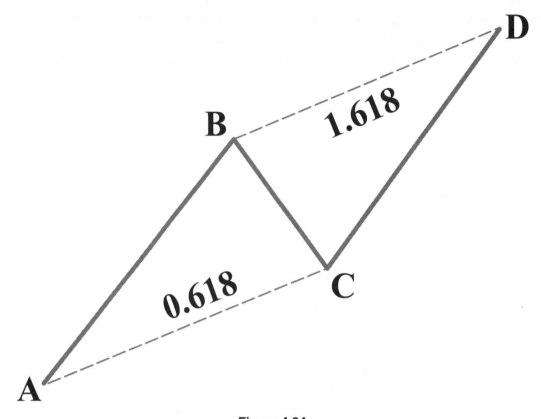

Figure 4.24

The AB=CD completion point should be the highest number in the PRZ and converge in a precise area as the 1.618 BC projection. The C point must be at a 0.618 retracement, which also establishes the reciprocal 1.618 BC projection. The perfect Bearish AB=CD pattern is an excellent harmonic setup that frequently develops on intra-day time frames. In many of the futures markets, a perfect Bearish AB=CD commonly marks intra-day highs.

Standard and Poor's 500 March 2010 Mini-Contract (ES_H0): 60-Minute

This perfect Bearish AB=CD defined a tight PRZ on the 60-minute chart (see Figure 4.25). The symmetry of the structure was perfect, as the ES formed this pattern with each leg (AB) requiring 18 days to complete.

Figure 4.25

The next chart of the price action in the PRZ shows the sharp reversal from the completion of this pattern (see Figure 4.26). It is important to note that the AB=CD completion point at 1119 was the defining limit in the PRZ. In a perfect Bearish AB=CD, the completion point of the AB=CD should sit above the 1.618 XA projection.

Figure 4.26

In this case, the numbers that defined the PRZ completed precisely at the same price level.

The AB=CD Pattern Summary

Although the basic AB=CD structure may possess a variety of Fibonacci ratios, the concept of support or resistance at the completion of two distinct and consecutive price legs is the essence of all harmonic patterns.

Alternate AB=CD patterns underscore the importance of using the basic structure to define the completion of specific patterns. In either AB=CD, the BC projection should complement the completion point of the pattern. It is important to remember the reciprocal relationships of the C point to the BC projection. A perfect AB=CD utilizes the 0.618 retracement and 1.618 extension, as the most harmonic alignment of Fibonacci ratios for the pattern. I believe that this pattern should possess specific characteristics to be a valid harmonic structure and to define a trading opportunity:

1. **Minimum AB=CD completion where each price leg is equivalent.**
2. **C point retracement can vary between a 0.382 to a 0.886, although 0.618 is preferred.**
3. **BC projection can vary from 1.13 to 3.618 and depends upon the C point retracement.**
4. **Alternate AB=CD patterns exist.**

It is important to mention that many Fibonacci-related analysts have oversimplified this pattern in recent years. The idea of trading every AB=CD that completes is absurd. Many people who present this pattern as the "end-all-be-all" price structure fail to understand that AB=CDs require many other considerations to confirm and complement the completion point. Preferably, the structure should possess other Fibonacci retracements or projections. However, the most important concept is that the AB=CD is the basic structure of all harmonic patterns.

Chapter 5

The Bat Pattern

The Bat pattern is a precise harmonic pattern that I discovered in 2001. The Bat pattern is probably the most accurate pattern in the entire Harmonic Trading arsenal. The pattern possesses many distinct elements that define an excellent Potential Reversal Zone (PRZ). The pattern typically represents a deep retest of support or resistance that can frequently be quite sharp. Quick reversals from Bat pattern PRZs are common. In fact, valid reversals from Bat patterns frequently possess price action that is quite extreme.

The pattern incorporates the powerful 0.886 XA retracement, as the defining element in the PRZ. The B point retracement must be less than a 0.618, preferably a 0.50 or 0.382 of the XA leg. The most ideal B point alignment is the 50% retracement of the XA leg. The B point is one of the primary ways to differentiate a Bat from a Gartley pattern. If a pattern is forming and the B point aligns at a 0.50 of the XA leg, it is likely to be a Bat.

The Bat utilizes a BC projection that is at least 1.618. The BC projection can be as much as 2.618. However, the most ideal BC projections in a Bat pattern are a 1.618 or a 2.0. It is important to note that the BC projection must not be a 1.27, as anything less than a 1.618 BC projection invalidates the structure. Furthermore, the 1.27 BC projections are usually found in Gartley structures.

The AB=CD pattern within the Bat distinguishes the structure, as well. This pattern is usually extended and ideally possesses a 1.27 AB=CD calculation in the Bat structure. However, the equivalent AB=CD pattern does serve as a minimum requirement for any Bat to be a valid setup.

The Bat is an incredibly accurate pattern and requires a smaller stop loss than most patterns. The 0.886 retracement is the most important number in the PRZ, but it is common for the other harmonic numbers within the structure to converge closely, defining in a precise range.

Bat Pattern Elements:

- **B point at a less than a 0.618 retracement of XA, preferably a distinct 50% or 38.2% retracement.**
- **BC projection must be at least 1.618.**
- **AB=CD pattern is usually extended.**
- **0.886 XA retracement.**
- **C point with range between 0.382 and 0.886.**

The Bullish Bat Pattern

A B point that is less than a 0.618 retracement, preferably a 0.50 or 0.382 of the XA leg, defines the Bullish Bat pattern (see Figure 5.1). The bullish 0.886 retracement is critical in this setup. Typically, Bullish Bat patterns are excellent 5-point corrective structures found in well-established support levels.

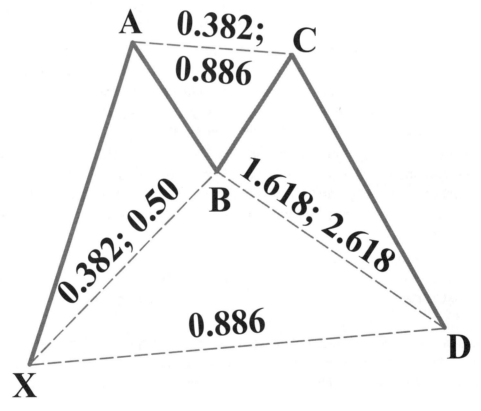

Figure 5.1

British Pound (GBP_A0-FX): 15-Minute

This first example of the British Pound shows a distinct Bullish Bat pattern with a precise PRZ (see Figure 5.2). The ratio alignment was quite precise, especially the 50% B point and extended BC projection. The three numbers of the PRZ defined a tight zone between 1.6242–1.6218 to get long. Specifically, the setup possessed a 1.618 AB=CD pattern at 1.6232, a 1.618 BC projection at 1.6218, and the 0.886 retracement at 1.6242.

Figure 5.2

In addition to an ideal alignment of Fibonacci numbers at the pattern's completion, the price structure possessed distinct symmetry that formed on this intra-day chart and provided a clear short-term trading opportunity. The chart in Figure 5.3 of the price action in the PRZ shows the near-perfect reversal on the first test of this support. After the price action tested the entire PRZ, the Pound bounced sharply from this area. The GBP bottomed 2 pips below the entire PRZ and reversed nicely for the next several hours, confirming the new intra-day up trend.

Figure 5.3

This example is an ideal scenario. A distinct Bullish Bat pattern with a sharp reversal from the PRZ is exactly the type of price action to expect in a valid harmonic setup. This pattern possessed all of the ideal elements for a valid buy signal. Again, the key technical event occurs immediately after the entire zone is tested. In this case, the Pound was clearly stabilizing at the numbers and decisively changed direction after the pattern was complete. Not to mention, the tight alignment of numbers in the PRZ and distinctively symmetrical pattern structure were further confirmation of an extremely harmonic setup.

Dow Jones Industrial Average (^DJI): Weekly

Figure 5.4 shows a Bullish Bat that was incredibly significant, as the reversal from this pattern marked the beginning of the 2003 bull market (see Figure 5.4). This weekly chart shows three numbers that defined a tight zone in the 7400–7500 area. The pattern possessed a 1.618 AB=CD pattern at 7500, while the 2.24 BC projection and the 0.886 retracement converged just under the 7400 mark.

Figure 5.4

As a side note, this pattern was extremely significant, and it was the deciding factor for my switch from a 2½ year bearish position on the index for my website advisory service. The sharp reversal from this PRZ and the distinct structure clearly indicated the strength of this pattern.

This chart of the price action in the PRZ (see Figure 5.5) shows the sharp reversal from the completion of this pattern. It is important to note that the 0.886 retracement at 7400 was the defining limit in the PRZ. In fact, the Dow Jones Industrial Average reversed almost exactly from this retracement.

Figure 5.5

The Alternate 1.618 AB=CD complemented the other numbers in the PRZ. This situation underscores the ability of the Bullish Bat to serve as a powerful 5-point corrective structure and define precise technical levels within the overall trend.

Swiss Franc
(CHF_A0-FX): 60-Minute

The next example of a Bullish Bat in the Swiss Franc shows another excellent harmonic pattern at well-defined support in the currency markets (see Figure 5.6). The 60-minute chart possessed a distinct pattern, clearly defining the critical support. The pattern formed the required Fibonacci alignment to validate the Bat structure and the price action stabilized nicely after testing the entire PRZ. The pattern marked an important continuation of the predominant intra-day trend.

Figure 5.6

These situations occur frequently in all currency markets on all time frames. Distinct patterns such as the example of the Swiss Franc are common, but it is important to wait for the clearest structural setups. Although the pattern possessed three numbers in a somewhat wide 50 pip range, the 0.886 retracement defined the extreme limit of the PRZ. Furthermore, the clear stabilization after all the numbers were tested was another signal of a valid reversal in the works.

Figure 5.7 of the Potential Reversal Zone is another example of ideal price action that validated the reversal. The well-defined projected harmonic support held firm, as the pattern's completion point was an excellent entry level for any long positions seeking to capitalize on a resuming bullish trend. Although patterns within trends will be addressed later in this material, it is important to know that valid structural signals commonly form in the middle of well-established trends. Although the relative position of all patterns should be considered, the price action after all the numbers in the PRZ are tested is still the most important technical consideration.

Figure 5.7

Another aspect of this example is the severity of the price decline toward the PRZ—although the preferred completion point with respect to time would have been more ideal if the price action tested the support zone a bit more steadily. The CD leg declined sharply in the hours leading up to the pattern's completion. Despite the somewhat premature test of the PRZ, the structure was still distinct and a valid setup.

This situation underscores the importance of PRICE over TIME. I would like to take a moment to comment on this controversy. Technicians have argued the "price versus time" debate for decades. Although time is an important element in many approaches of Technical Analysis, I believe the emphasis within the realm of Harmonic Trading must be focused on price measurements. I utilize time measurements with respect to patterns. In fact, the Harmonic Analyzer is able to calculate effective time projections that complement harmonic pattern structures. But, the time element of any technical method must include price as the primary basis for trading decisions.

Goldman Sachs (GS): Daily

Figure 5.8 is an example of a Bullish Bat in Goldman Sachs that shows a distinct PRZ that utilizes an equivalent AB=CD pattern. It is important to note that the equivalent AB=CD is a minimum target in the PRZ of a Bat pattern. The stock possessed the necessary Fibonacci alignments to validate the Bat structure, including a 1.618 BC projection and a 0.886 retracement. The chart in Figure 5.9 of the price action in the PRZ shows the sharp reversal from the completion of this pattern.

Figure 5.8

Figure 5.9

The stock rallied convincingly after testing all of the numbers in the PRZ. Again, it is important to note that the 0.886 retracement just above 61 was the defining limit in the PRZ, and it should be considered as the most important number in the completion of the pattern.

Chevron-Texaco (CVX): Daily

The next example of Chevron-Texaco shows a distinct Bullish Bat pattern that formed on the daily chart (see Figure 5.10). The stock possessed the necessary Fibonacci alignments to validate the Bat structure, especially the precise 50% B point. The stock reversed after testing the entire range of the PRZ. Although the reversal occurred immediately after hitting the completion point, this distinct pattern clearly identified a buying opportunity just under the $60.

Figure 5.10

The chart in Figure 5.11 of the price action in the PRZ shows the sharp reversal after testing the entire range of the PRZ. The 0.886 retracement converged exactly in the same area as the 2.0 BC projection, and the Bullish Alternate 1.618 AB=CD projection at 56.50. Although the Alternate AB=CD was 2 points below the other two numbers, this example underscores the importance of each number in the PRZ. The stock rallied convincingly after testing the entire PRZ and confirmed the reversal within a few days after the initial test of the setup

Figure 5.11

Although some situations can be more difficult to gauge than others, this example demonstrates the importance of focusing on the entire range of the PRZ. In this case, Chevron-Texaco possessed harmonic support just under the $60 level with the completion of the Bullish Bat. As the stock fell under $60, the price action appeared to be quite severe. However, Chevron-Texaco soon stabilized and reversed course after testing the PRZ. Even if the execution was delayed a day or two, the pattern clearly marked a critical turning point for the stock and defined an optimal entry for a long position within the overall trend of the price action.

The Bearish Bat Pattern

A B point that is less than a 0.618 retracement, preferably a 0.50 or 0.382 of the XA leg, defines the Bearish Bat pattern (see Figure 5.12). Bearish Bat patterns are excellent 5-point corrective structures that frequently form after retracing a critical high point. In addition, these structures are excellent trading opportunities when they form at distinct levels of resistance.

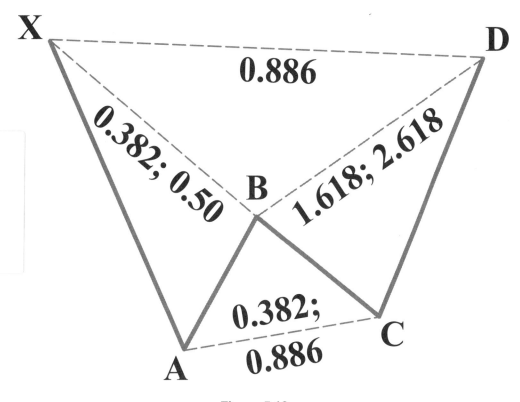

Figure 5.12

The 0.886 XA retracement is the most critical level in the Bearish Bat. Since this retracement occurs close to the prior high—which is the initial starting point (X) of the pattern—the price action represents a substantial challenge of prior resistance. The structural signal that the Bat pattern represents is a substantial technical factor that must be considered more significant than simple retests. Bat patterns that form at distinct levels of resistance frequently indicate substantial potential changes in trend—on any timeframe! It is important to wait for clear opportunities like these. Not to mention, I prefer to wait for the entire PRZ range to be tested to validate the completion of the pattern. Although this may delay a trade execution slightly, valid reversals will provide definitive signals soon after the pattern is completed.

J. P. Morgan (JPM): Weekly

J. P. Morgan Chase formed a distinct Bearish Bat on this weekly chart with a precise PRZ in the $48 area (see Figure 5.13). The pattern possessed three numbers that defined a tight zone between 47.20–48.05 to short the stock.

Figure 5.13

The pattern possessed a 1.618 AB=CD that converged in the same area as the 2.0 BC projection. The 0.886 retracement at 47.70 was the defining upside limit for this setup, as the stock reversed quickly after testing the entire PRZ.

The chart in Figure 5.14 of the price action in the PRZ shows an ideal reversal after the 0.886 retracement was tested. Ideally, the entire PRZ should be tested in valid reversals. In fact, the Bearish Bat tends to test its entire PRZ in valid structures more than most other patterns. This is different from other 5-point corrective structures like the Gartley, where a less strict approach is employed with the price action in the PRZ.

Figure 5.14

This case of JPM exemplifies the advantage of waiting for an entire test of the Bat PRZ. The stock rallied into the range of harmonic numbers between 47.20 and 48 as it completely tested the PRZ and confirmed the ultimate reversal at 0.886 retracement. The following few weeks confirmed the reversal, as the sock rolled immediately after completing the Bat pattern.

Eurodollar (EUR_A0-FX): 60-Minute

This Bearish Bat in the Euro illustrates an ideal structural scenario, where the pattern's completion point serves as the optimal entry level for a trade (see Figure 5.15). The ideal symmetry and precise alignment of the structure's ratios clearly validated the pattern.

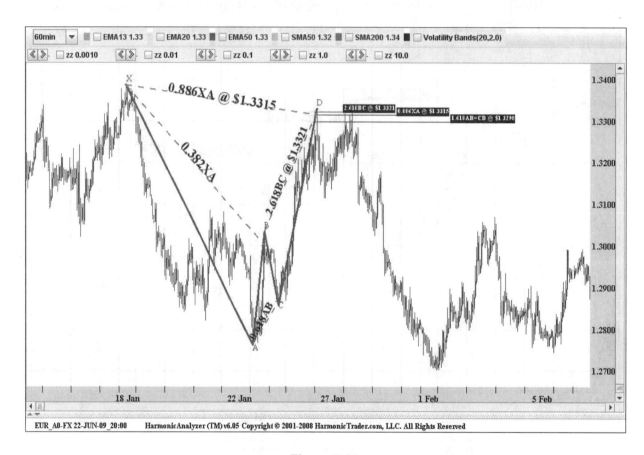

Figure 5.15

The price action reversed from the entire test of the PRZ. After a temporary pullback from the initial test, the Euro consolidated within the range of harmonic resistance between 1.4419 and 1.4437, and reversed *after* a second test of the entire PRZ. Again, the 0.886 retracement in the 1.4437 area was the defining limit of the pattern and the most significant number in the zone. In addition, the 0.886 retracement is typically the optimal area to execute a trade, as was the case for the Euro. The chart in Figure 5.16 shows the price action in the PRZ. Despite the strong rally that preceded the PRZ, the clear stalling that occurred after testing the harmonic resistance validated the Bearish Bat pattern.

Figure 5.16

After rallying several hundred pips, the Euro formed a sharp Bearish Bat that not only reversed at the completion of the pattern, but topped at nearly the exact high end of the PRZ. The initial test yielded a valid short-term reversal. The more substantial move required a secondary test and further consolidation before reversing dramatically. After consolidating in this area, the Euro actually formed a smaller Bearish Bat on the secondary test (see Figure 5.17). This "pattern within a pattern" is just one of many types of multi-harmonic scenarios that should be regarded as an additional structural confirmation of the setup. In this case, the convergence of multi-patterns can have much greater implications for the reversal zone as a critical turning point for the potential future trend. The smaller Bearish Bat completed at 1.3325, which is the same level as the larger 88.6% retracement completes. The reversal following this secondary test was a clear confirmation signal of the validity of these patterns as critical harmonic resistance.

Figure 5.17

Although multiple harmonic patterns do not occur in every situation, it is common for many valid reversals to experience some type of secondary test of significant setups before reversing decisively. In fact, it is common to experience some type of reaction on the first test of an entire PRZ. After some meaningful consolidation, a nominal retest of the PRZ often occurs that marks the beginning of the reversal acceleration. These situations are excellent trading opportunities because they provide ample time to analyze the price action and to execute the trade.

Coca-Cola (KO): Weekly

Coca-Cola in Figure 5.18 shows a long-term Bearish Bat on this weekly chart. The pattern possessed a precise PRZ with three numbers that defined a tight range zone between 34.55 and 36.30 (see Figure 5.17). The stock reversed after testing the entire PRZ (again) with the 0.886 retracement acting as the defining number within this range.

Figure 5.18

This example illustrates the ideal alignment that valid Bat patterns typically possess. The exact 50% B point retracement with the Alternate 1.27 AB=CD pattern and the 2.0 BC projection were ideal structural elements that defined this precise PRZ. Although the 0.886 was the defining element of this setup, the other two levels complemented this area ideally. Figure 5.19 reveals the clear reversal that unfolded after a complete test of all of the numbers in the zone.

Figure 5.19

The remarkable aspect of this example is the length of time required to form this structure. This pattern formed over a period of seven years and incredibly the uptrend reversed on the week it hit the completion point.

The Perfect Bat Pattern

The perfect Bat pattern is represented by a specific alignment of Fibonacci numbers within the structure. The perfect Bat is a distinct structure with a tight range of three numbers that defines the Potential Reversal Zone (PRZ). The mid-point is primarily defined by an exact 0.50% B point retracement. The Alternate 1.27 AB=CD and the 2.0 BC projection should complete close to the 0.886 retracement, which is the most critical number in the pattern.

Perfect Bat Pattern Requirements:

1. **Mandatory 50% B point retracement of the XA leg.**
2. **Precise 0.886 D point retracement of the XA leg as the defining limit within the PRZ.**
3. **2.0 BC projection.**
4. **Alternate 1.27 AB=CD pattern required.**
5. **C point should be in the 50–61.8% range.**

The Perfect Bullish Bat

The perfect Bullish Bat pattern is primarily defined by a precise 50% retracement at the B point (see Figure 5.20). The PRZ must possess an 0.886 retracement as the defining limit, and this area should be complemented by a 2.0 BC projection with an Alternate 1.27 AB=CD pattern. It is important to point out that the "0.50; 0.618" Fibonacci retracement range for the C point is the only "discretionary alignment" permitted. This C point range is the most ideal retracement to establish a 2.0 BC projection.

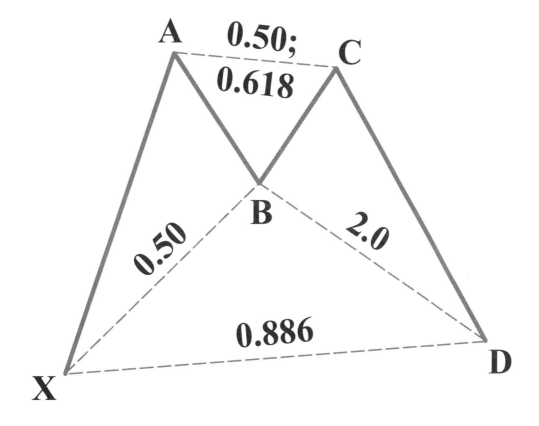

Figure 5.20

Intel (INTC): 60-Minute

The intra-day example of the Intel in Figure 5.21 shows a perfect Bullish Bat pattern with a precise Potential Reversal Zone (PRZ). The ratio alignment was quite precise, especially the 50% B point and extended BC projection. The three numbers of the PRZ defined a tight zone in the 15.80 area to get long. Specifically, the setup possessed a 1.27 AB=CD pattern at 15.75, with the 2.0 BC projection and the 0.886 retracement competing at 15.80.

Figure 5.21

In addition to an ideal alignment of Fibonacci ratios to validate the perfect structure, the pattern's distinct symmetry was another ideal element of this short-term setup. The chart in Figure 5.22 of the price action in the PRZ shows the near-perfect reversal on the first test of this support. After the price action entered the PRZ, the price action stabilized and reversed from the 88.6% retracement. The stock rallied decisively over the next several sessions to confirm the new intra-day up trend.

Figure 5.22

This example exhibits an ideal scenario. A distinct Bullish Bat pattern with a sharp reversal from the PRZ is exactly the type of price action to expect in a valid harmonic setup. This pattern possessed all the ideal elements for a valid buy signal. Not to mention, the tight alignment of numbers in the PRZ and distinctively symmetrical pattern structure was further confirmation of an extremely harmonic setup.

The Perfect Bearish Bat

The perfect Bearish Bat pattern is primarily defined by an exact 0.50 retracement at the B point. The PRZ must possess an 0.886 retracement as the defining upper limit, and this area should be complemented by a 2.0 BC projection with an alternate 1.27 AB=CD pattern (see Figure 5.23).

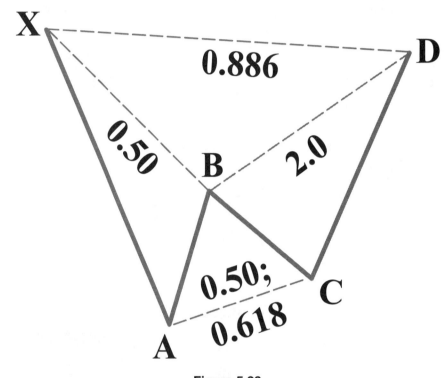

Figure 5.23

It is important to point out that the "0.50; 0.618" Fibonacci retracement range for the C point is the only "discretionary alignment" permitted. This C point range is the most ideal retracement to establish a 2.0 BC projection.

NASDAQ 100 Tracking Stock (QQQQ): 5-Minute

The Bearish Bat in this example possesses a perfect structure with a precise alignment of the required Fibonacci ratios to validate the pattern. Starting with a perfect 50% B point retracement, the price action formed an Alternate 1.27 AB=CD pattern that completed in the same exact area as the 2.0 BC projection. In combination with the 0.886 XA retracement, the PRZ possessed three numbers in a 10-cent range that defined resistance just above $30 a share.

The chart in Figure 5.24 clearly demonstrates the effectiveness of the perfect pattern structure to define critical turning points within any trend. In this case, the perfect Bearish Bat defined an optimal execution area to short the Qs.

Figure 5.24

The Bat Pattern Summary

The Bat pattern is a precise harmonic pattern that frequently yields exact and sharp reversals. The 0.886 retracement is a powerful completion point and the defining limit within the PRZ. Although a 0.50 or 0.382 retracement is preferred, any B point that is less than a 0.618 will define a valid Bat structure. The Bat pattern incorporates a minimum AB=CD completion to validate the structure, as well. However, an Alternate 1.27 AB=CD is most common and is a defining element in the Perfect Bat structure. Furthermore, the BC projection should complement the other numbers in the PRZ, and it must be at least a 1.618 extension.

1. **B point retracement of the XA leg must be less than 0.618 with a 0.50 or 0.382 retracement preferred.**
2. **Precise 0.886 D point retracement of the XA leg as the defining limit within the PRZ.**
3. **Minimum 1.618 BC projection with extreme extensions (2.0–2.618) possible.**
4. **Minimum AB=CD completion, although an Alternate 1.27 AB=CD is more common and preferred.**
5. **C point retracement can vary between a 0.382 to an 0.886.**

The Bat pattern is probably the best harmonic pattern of them all! Bat structures represent powerful corrective signals that identify excellent trading opportunities that are retesting significant levels of support or resistance. The best structures typically are distinct and possess a precise alignment of Fibonacci ratios to validate the pattern.

Chapter 6

The Gartley Pattern

The Great Gartley Controversy

It is probably the best-known Harmonic pattern in the trading community—the Gartley. Although many have written articles on this pattern, the origins of the Gartley pattern range from erroneous to downright misinformation. H. M. Gartley first outlined the basic structure of this pattern in his book *Profits in the Stock Market* (Lambert-Gann Publishing, 1935) on page 222. Although contrary to what many have claimed, Gartley was *not* responsible for assigning Fibonacci ratios to this price structure. In fact, *Profits in the Stock Market* did not mention anything about Fibonacci ratios in the entire book. I know because I own the book. It's not in there. I believe it is important to correct these prevailing misconceptions regarding this pattern.

It is important to note that others have assigned a variety of Fibonacci ratios to the framework of the Gartley pattern. However, they have used a large gamut of Fibonacci numbers at the D points, essentially labeling any AB=CD pattern as a Gartley. This interpretation assumes that any reversal is valid if it completes at a 0.618 or a 0.786 without regard for the overall structural alignment. This has created much confusion among the technical community and has challenged the reputation of the pattern.

This controversy was one of the earliest challenges that I faced when I initially refined the pattern. I argued with many people that "all Gartley patterns are not the same." If anything, the most effective Gartley pattern required an exact specification of Fibonacci ratios to validate the structure. Although the general structure has been outlined previously, it was not until *The Harmonic Trader* was released in 1999 that the exact rules for specific retracements of the B point at a 0.618 and the D point at a 0.786 were to be assigned to the pattern. This alignment has now become the standard in the technical community and is now commonly referred to as the Gartley pattern.

The exact 0.618 B point requirement was just one condition in this interpretation of the structure. *The Harmonic Trader* also outlined the importance of the AB=CD pattern and the BC projection rules that required specific conditions to validate the structure.

The Potential Reversal Zone (PRZ) of a Gartley possesses several other elements that differentiate the structure from other patterns. The pattern should possess a distinct and equivalent AB=CD pattern that converges in the same area as the 0.786 XA retracement. In fact, the completion of the equivalent AB=CD pattern and the 0.786 retracement are minimum requirements for a valid Gartley. Frequently, the 0.786 XA retracement overlaps the AB=CD in the PRZ. In these cases, this convergence typically represents the defining level of the PRZ.

The BC projection is another specific condition to validate the structure, and it must not exceed a 1.618. Although the BC projection is a less significant number in the PRZ than in other patterns, the 1.618 limit helps to differentiate the Gartley structure. Typically, a BC extension greater than a 1.618 is found in Bat structures. Regardless of the required numbers in the PRZ, the Gartley must possess a precise 0.618 B point retracement to validate the structure. In fact, the Gartley pattern requires the most precise B point alignment of all the harmonic patterns to define the best trading opportunities.

Gartley Pattern Elements:

- **Precise 61.8% B point retracement of XA leg.**
- **BC projection must not exceed 1.618.**
- **Equivalent AB=CD pattern is most common.**
- **0.786 XA retracement.**
- **C point within range of 0.382–0.886 retracement.**

It has been my experience that anything less than the ideal Fibonacci alignment for the Gartley usually results in "deeper" corrective structures, favoring a Bat pattern completion. Although this strict application of the Gartley alignment reduces the number of pattern matches, it is critical in identifying valid patterns and effectively differentiating these two similar structures.

It is important to note that the Gartley pattern is simply one type of "M" or "W" Elliott Wave corrective pattern. Although similar in structure, the Bat pattern is a distinctly different entity, utilizing other rules to define the setup. Such specification of price structures, quantified by Fibonacci calculations, is essential in Harmonic Trading. In terms of the Gartley pattern, the setup that yields the most valid reversals is the one illustrated in *The Harmonic Trader*.

As with all harmonic patterns, the specification of Fibonacci points within each structure is extremely critical in determining valid trading opportunities. The Gartley pattern exemplifies the necessity of such specification, as the structure frequently resembles a Bat pattern as it completes.

On a final note about harmonic patterns, *The Harmonic Trader* outlined many unprecedented strategies that distinguished patterns based upon specific price point alignments. This differentiation increased the effectiveness and served to demystify the confusion of the overall application of these methods. Again, I must emphasize that although others have utilized a variety of Fibonacci numbers in their analysis of price patterns, the exact specification of price structures, quantified by Fibonacci calculations, is what separates Harmonic Trading from the rest.

The Bullish Gartley

A distinct AB=CD and a 0.786 retracement define the Potential Reversal Zone (PRZ) in the Bullish Gartley (see Figure 6.1). However, these conditions are valid only with a 0.618 B point retracement of the XA leg.

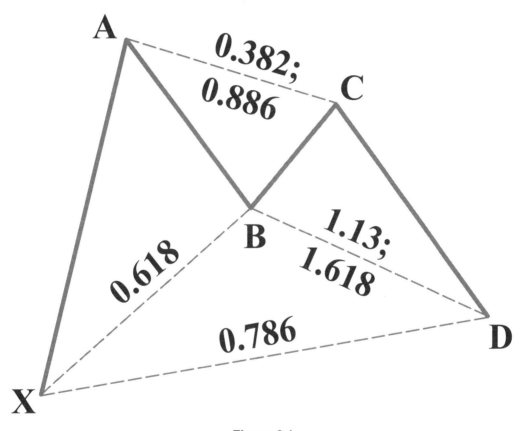

Figure 6.1

The BC projection should complement the other numbers in the PRZ, as a 1.13, 1.27, 1.41, or 1.618 extension should converge in the same area. It is important to note that the Gartley does not utilize any BC projection that is greater than a 1.618. Any BC projection that is greater than a 1.618 is usually found in Bat structures. Again, it is important to point out that the "0.382;0.886" Fibonacci retracement range for the C point can be any of the Harmonic Trading ratios that fall between these two constraints. Therefore, the C point can be 0.382, 0.50, 0.618, 0.707, 0.786, or 0.886.

Newmont Mining (NEM): Weekly

This first example of a weekly chart of Newmont Mining (NEM) illustrates the ideal Bullish Gartley elements (see Figure 6.2). Starting with a precise 0.618 B point alignment to validate the structure, the distinct AB=CD pattern completion point at 19.30 converged closely with the 0.786 XA retracement at 19.35. The 1.41 BC projection complemented this area at 18.70. Although this area was exceeded slightly, the pattern clearly indicated harmonic support around the $19 level.

Figure 6.2

The chart in Figure 6.3 of the price action in the PRZ shows an ideal reversal after the 1.41 BC projection was tested. The interesting aspect of this reversal is the stabilization that occurred after the 0.786 and the AB=CD completion points were tested. Although Newmont Mining required several weeks of consolidation before reversing, the Bullish Gartley accurately identified critical support for the stock.

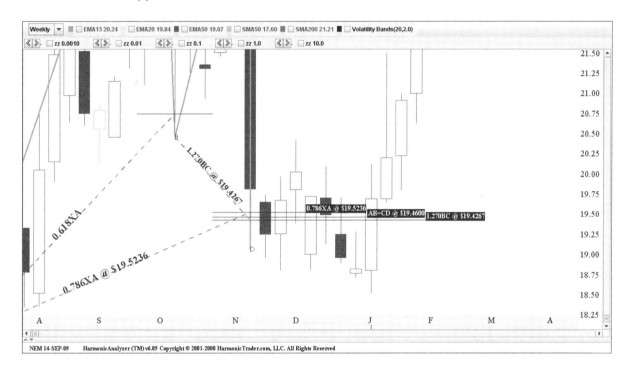

Figure 6.3

Although this concept may sound repetitive, it is important to emphasize the difference of a Gartley structure versus a Bat pattern. The most important element that differentiates this 5-point corrective structure from a Bat pattern is the B point retracement at the 0.618 level of the XA leg. If this was a Bat structure—defined by a 0.50 B point retracement or less, the corresponding BC projection and Alternate 1.27 AB=CD pattern would have calculated a lower PRZ, resulting in a missed trade.

Standard and Poor's 500 June 2003 Mini-Contract (ES_M9): 5-Minute

The ES formed a distinct Bullish Gartley on this 5-minute chart. This was a nice structure with an ideal alignment of harmonic numbers that defined a distinct intra-day PRZ in the 920 area. (see Figure 6.4).

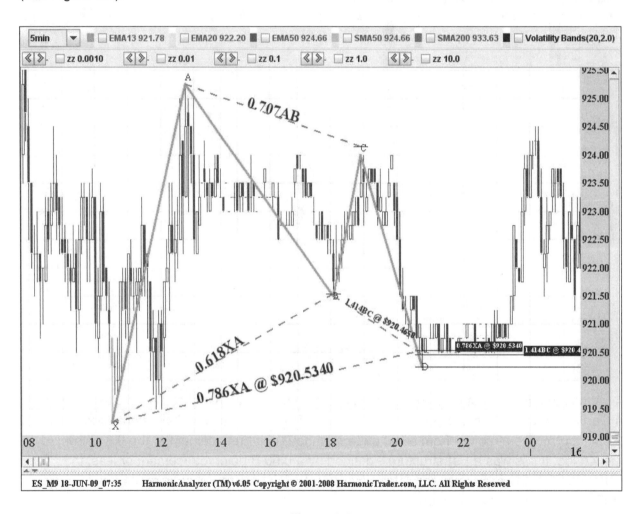

Figure 6.4

The overlapping of the AB=CD and the 0.786 retracement defined the critical area within the PRZ, as the ES reversed sharply after testing this area. It is important to emphasize the convergence of these two numbers in the Gartley PRZ. Although I prefer to wait for the entire range of harmonic numbers to be tested in most patterns, the Gartley frequently reverses after testing the AB=CD completion point and the 0.786 retracement. Not to mention, the convergence of these numbers at the 920 level clearly defined critical intra-day harmonic support.

NASDAQ 100 September 2003 Mini-Contract (NQ_U3): Daily

The September 2003 NQ Mini-contract formed this distinct Bullish Gartley on the daily chart, marking the beginning of a huge rally. This pattern possessed a distinct structure with an ideal alignment of harmonic numbers that defined a distinct PRZ between 1203.40 and 1213.50 (see Figure 6.5).

Figure 6.5

The convergence of the AB=CD completion point and the 0.786 XA retracement were the defining elements of the PRZ, as the contract reversed sharply after testing this area. Although the 1.41 BC projection complemented the PRZ, it was not tested. This exemplifies the importance of the AB=CD and the 0.786 XA retracement in the PRZ for the Gartley pattern.

Dow Jones Industrial Average Tracking Stock (DIA): Daily

The Dow Diamonds formed this Bullish Gartley on the daily chart (see Figure 6.6) with three numbers in a tight range between 118–120. The pattern possessed a distinct structure with a perfect 0.618 B point retracement.

Figure 6.6

This was another situation where the Gartley PRZ was defined by the convergence of the AB=CD completion point and the 0.786 XA retracement. Although the BC projection marked the low at $118, the convergence of the AB=CD completion and the 0.786 retracement identified the most important area in the PRZ between. This was an important structural pattern for the Dow Diamonds, as it confirmed the critical bear market low.

Microsoft (MSFT): 60-Minute

After a severe decline, Microsoft consolidated over the course of several sessions to form a distinct Gartley on this 60-minute chart (see Figure 6.7).

Figure 6.7

The B point retracement reversed close to the 0.618 XA retracement, establishing the structure of the pattern. The AB=CD completion point, the 0.786 XA retracement, and the 1.41 BC projection converged in a tight 10-cent range between 23.15–23.25. The stock rallied in the following two weeks after the entire PRZ was tested.

The Bearish Gartley Pattern

The Bearish Gartley structure is principally identified by a 0.618 B point retracement of the XA leg (see Figure 6.8). The other elements of the pattern—the AB=CD, the BC projection, and the 0.786 retracement—should converge within close proximity of each other to define the PRZ.

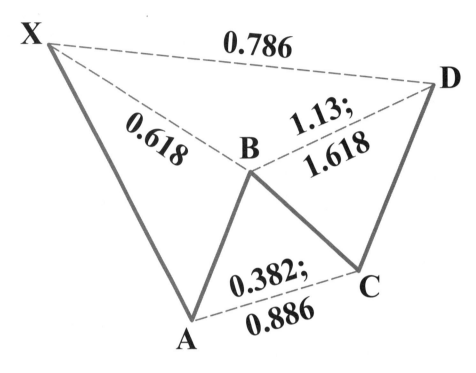

Figure 6.8

Standard and Poor's 500 Index (^SPX): Weekly

This first example of a Bearish Gartley was incredibly significant for the financial markets. The Standard and Poor's 500 Index completed this Bearish Gartley on the weekly chart at the index's all-time high, marking the beginning of the three-year bear market. The distinct AB=CD pattern completion point and the 0.786 XA retracement were complemented by the 1.27 BC projection, defining the area just above the 1500 level as critical resistance (see Figure 6.9).

Although the price action exceeded the top end of the range, the reversal occurred the week after the price action tested the entire range of the PRZ.

The chart in Figure 6.10 shows an ideal reversal after this complete test.

The action after the entire PRZ was tested exemplifies an ideal reversal of a valid pattern. In this case, the S&P 500 stalled at this harmonic resistance and continued lower in the weeks following the reversal.

Figure 6.9

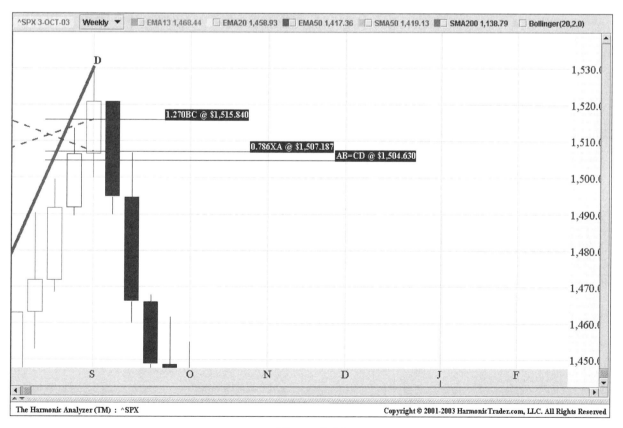

Figure 6.10

Swiss Franc (CHF_A0-FX): 60-Minute

The next example of a Bearish Gartley in the Swiss Franc shows another excellent harmonic pattern in the currency markets (see Figure 6.11). The 60-minute chart possessed a distinct pattern, clearly defining the critical harmonic resistance. The pattern formed the required Fibonacci alignment to validate the structure, especially the precise 0.618 B point. The price action stabilized nicely after testing the entire PRZ and the pattern represented an excellent intra-day selling opportunity.

Figure 6.11

Although the 0.786 XA retracement and the 1.618 BC projection converged in the low range of the zone, the reversal did not occur until the AB=CD was completed. Again, this example underscores the importance of the AB=CD pattern as a mandatory requirement in the Gartley PRZ. The following chart of the price action in the PRZ shows the resistance as defined by the AB=CD completion point (see Figure 6.12).

Figure 6.12

The price action clearly stalled in the zone and rolled over decisively after testing all the numbers at the pattern's completion point. The distinct structure provided a clear signal of an impending reversal. These situations materialize in all markets on any timeframe. However, harmonic patterns in the currency markets frequently provide even more defined opportunities, as these intra-day setups continually materialize. Although smaller intra-day intervals provide similar trading opportunities, the larger patterns on 15-minute and 60-minute timeframes tend to allow for more deliberation and to offer clearer reversal signals.

United States Oil Fund ETF (USO): 15-Minute

The USO formed a Bearish Gartley on this 60-minute chart (see Figure 6.13). The distinct AB=CD pattern completion point and the 0.786 XA retracement defined the 44 area as critical intra-day resistance. The price action reversed immediately after testing all the numbers in the PRZ. The AB=CD pattern defined the top range of the resistance and confirmed the optimal entry point for the trade. Again, it is important to note that the distinguishing element of this example is the precise 0.618 B point retracement that validated the structure.

Figure 6.13

The following chart of the price action in the PRZ shows an ideal reversal after the AB=CD and the 0.786 XA retracement were tested (see Figure 6.14). The interesting aspect of this reversal is the downside continuation that occurred after the reversal was complete. However, the quick test that occurred at the pattern's completion could have resulted in a missed opportunity. When the price action traded into the PRZ, it reversed on the open of the next day's trading.

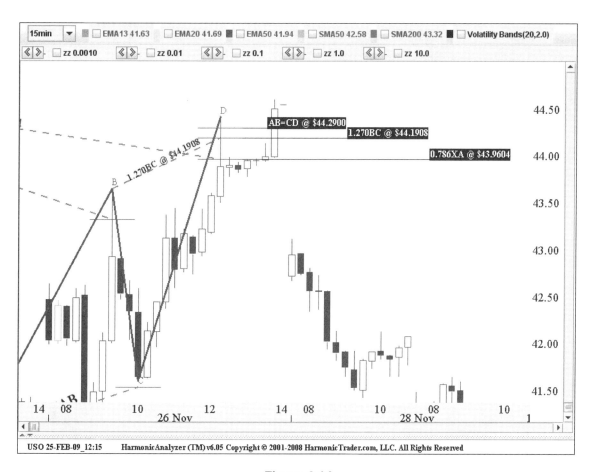

Figure 6.14

Although execution techniques will be covered later in this book in Chapter 11, "The Harmonic Trade Management System," this example underscores the importance of executing in the zone. The Bearish Gartley pattern clearly indicated the area just above the $44 level as the ideal entry for the short. When the price action hit the zone, there was a distinct window of opportunity to execute the trade.

As I mentioned in the previous chapter, this is another example of the importance of PRICE over TIME. Without engaging into a long-winded debate, the importance of price targets as a determination for the execution of a trade must outweigh the time projections and expectations of the market action. In the case of the USO, the focus should have been on the completion point of the AB=CD pattern.

New Zealand Dollar (NZD_A0-FX): 15-Minute

The next example in the New Zealand Dollar illustrates the ideal structure that valid Bearish Gartley patterns should possess. The distinct harmonic pattern on the 15-minute chart in Figure 6.15 defined another fantastic intra-day trading opportunity in the currency markets. The setup identified critical harmonic resistance in the 0.5330 area. The pattern formed the required Fibonacci alignment to validate the structure, with a precise 0.618 B point in particular. The price action stalled after testing the entire PRZ and reversed shortly thereafter.

Figure 6.15

Figure 6.16 shows the price action at the completion of the pattern. The rally stalled right at the numbers and reversed immediately after testing the PRZ. The distinct change in the nature of the preceding uptrend was the overwhelming sign that the reversal was valid. The execution of the short should focus on the entire range of the projected harmonic resistance, as this example presents an ideal scenario of price action that reverses ideally from the completion of the setup.

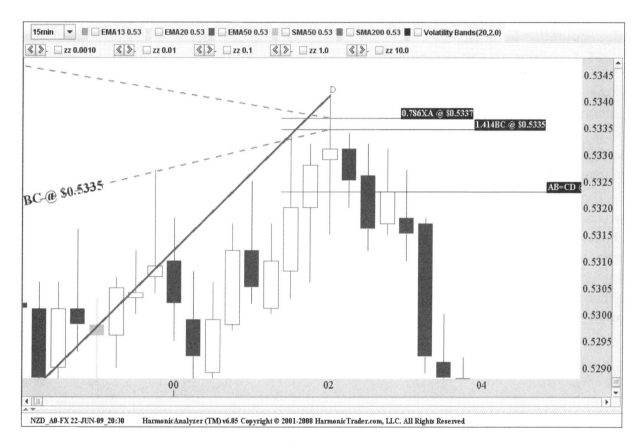

Figure 6.16

The Perfect Gartley

The Perfect Gartley should possess the following elements:

1. **Precise 0.618 B point retracement of the XA leg.**
2. **Precise 0.786 D point retracement of the XA leg in the PRZ.**
3. **Mandatory 1.618 BC projection.**
4. **Equivalent and Perfect AB=CD (0.618/1.618) with distinct symmetry and time duration for each leg.**
5. **C point at a 0.618 retracement.**

Although the *ideal* Gartley is well defined, a perfect Gartley utilizes the perfect AB=CD pattern (0.618/1.618) structure. The perfect AB=CD is primarily defined by the C point retracement that should be precisely 0.618 of the AB leg. The 0.618 C point retracement sets up the 1.618 BC projection. For obvious reasons, the 0.618 and 1.618 AB=CD pattern represent the most harmonic ratios that are directly derived from the Fibonacci sequence.

The perfect Gartley should entail an exact B point retracement. Although the ideal Gartley structure allows only a slight variation of the 0.618 B point retracement, a perfect Gartley should possess an almost exact retracement. Furthermore, the C point should be at a 0.618 retracement. Due to the perfect AB=CD required to validate this structure, the C point is another precise ratio that distinguishes the pattern. Another aspect of the perfect Gartley pattern is the general symmetry and time consideration of the structure, where each leg is exactly equivalent in duration.

The Perfect Bullish Gartley

The perfect Bullish Gartley pattern is primarily defined by an exact 0.618 retracement at the B point (see Figure 6.17). Although the ideal price action should test the entire range of the Potential Reversal Zone (PRZ), the minimum AB=CD and the 0.786 XA leg still represent the most important numbers in the completion pattern. The structure should be distinct and possess ideal symmetry. In addition, the AB=CD should be a perfect bullish structure with 0.618 and 1.618 ratios at the respective points. The combination of these elements define a remarkably ideal setup with a particularly critical PRZ. Although these structures are rare, they represent the best alignment of all the Gartley variations.

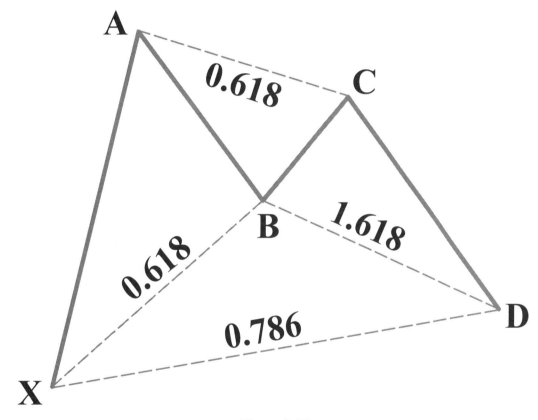

Figure 6.17

Standard and Poor's 500 Tracking Stock (SPY): 5-Minute

The following chart of the perfect Bullish Gartley in the SPY exemplifies the required structure and alignment of Fibonacci ratios to validate the pattern (see Figure 6.18). Starting with an almost exact 61.8% B point retracement, the price action formed a perfect AB=CD pattern that reversed exactly at the pattern's completion point.

Figure 6.18

The 0.786 XA retracement and the 1.618 BC projection complemented the perfect Bullish AB=CD pattern to define a tight Potential Reversal Zone (PRZ). These numbers clearly pinpointed the trade opportunity to buy the intra-day support in a close 15-cent range just under 87.50 level. Figure 6.19 of the price action in the PRZ shows an ideal reversal after all of the harmonic numbers were tested.

Figure 6.19

The SPY declined sharply as it approached the PRZ. Despite this drop, the price action stabilized shortly after the pattern completed and rallied significantly immediately after testing all of the numbers in the zone. In addition, the tight range of the PRZ created a clear make-or-break harmonic support that represented an optimal entry for the intra-day long position.

The Perfect Bearish Gartley

The perfect Bearish Gartley pattern is defined by an exact 0.618 retracement at the B point (see Figure 6.20). In addition, a perfect Bearish AB=CD and the 0.786 XA leg must be complemented by a 1.618 BC projection.

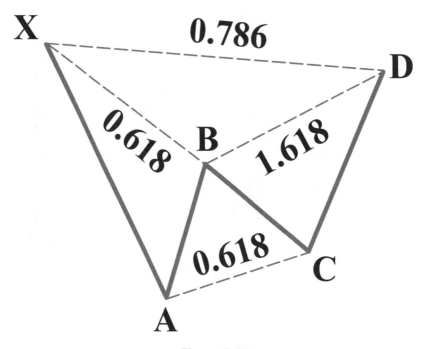

Figure 6.20

British Pound
(GBP_A0-FX): 15-Minute

The British Pound formed a perfect Bearish Gartley on 15-minute chart in Figure 6.21. The perfect Bullish AB=CD pattern completion point and the 0.786 XA retracement in the 1.3830 area were the defining limits in the PRZ, as the price action reversed immediately after testing these numbers. The 1.618 BC projection complemented the resistance and confirmed the optimal entry target for the trade. Again, it is important to note that the distinguishing element of this example is the precise 0.618 B point retracement that validated the structure.

Figure 6.21

The price action in the Potential Reversal Zone (PRZ) shows an ideal reversal after the AB=CD and the 0.786 XA retracement were tested. The interesting aspect of this reversal is the downside continuation that occurred after the reversal was complete. However, the quick test that occurred at the pattern's completion could have resulted in a missed opportunity. When the price action traded into the PRZ, it reversed immediately thereafter. Although execution techniques will be covered later in this book in the Trade Management section, this example underscores the importance of executing in the zone. The Bearish Gartley pattern clearly indicated the area at the 1.3830 level as the ideal entry for the short. When the stock hit the zone, there was only a small window of opportunity to execute the trade.

Gartley Pattern Summary

The Gartley pattern is a controversial pattern. Despite the varying interpretations within *The Great Gartley Controversy*, the most harmonic Gartley pattern possesses distinct characteristics at all points within the structural rules were originally outlined in "The Harmonic Trader."

The 0.618 B point retracement is critical in defining a valid Gartley structure. Although the 0.786 XA retracement is an important element of the structure, the equivalent AB=CD within the pattern is the most critical completion point in the Potential Reversal Zone (PRZ). Furthermore, the AB=CD completion is a mandatory minimum requirement for all valid Gartley patterns.

1. **Precise 0.618 B point retracement of the XA leg.**
2. **Precise 0.786 D point retracement of the XA leg in the PRZ.**
3. **1.27 or 1.618 BC projection.**
4. **Equivalent AB=CD.**
5. **C point retracement can vary between a 0.382 to a 0.886.**

The Gartley pattern must include these specific conditions to define the best harmonic structures. Although the Gartley may resemble a Bat, the Fibonacci ratios utilized in the setup are unique to this pattern. In addition, the pattern should be quite distinct and possess ideal symmetry.

Chapter 7

The Crab Pattern

The Crab is a precise harmonic pattern that I discovered in 2000. The Crab is a distinct 5-point extension structure that utilizes a 1.618 projection of the XA leg exclusively. This is the most critical aspect of the pattern and the defining level in the Potential Reversal Zone (PRZ). The extreme (2.618, 3.14, 3.618) projection of the BC complements the 1.618 XA extension. In addition, the Crab primarily utilizes an Alternate AB=CD to complement the PRZ. Although a minimum AB=CD completion is necessary for a valid structure, the Alternate 1.27 or 1.618 calculation are the most commonly found variations in the PRZ. In fact, the 1.618 AB=CD pattern is the most common alternate calculation utilized in the structure.

It is important to note that the alternate AB=CD pattern within the Crab is the least important number in the PRZ. The combination of the 1.618 projection of the XA leg and the extreme BC projection usually creates a distinct range for the completion of the pattern. In fact, the AB=CD calculation is probably the least important in the Crab than all other patterns. Although the AB=CD structure is less significant in the case of the Crab, the pattern should still possess a distinct symmetry.

Due to the extremity of the projections utilized in the completion of the pattern, the Crab frequently experiences sharp price action and dramatic reversals. It is common for price action to possess extreme ranges, quickly testing the Crab PRZ during the reversal. In fact, the price action experienced in Crab pattern completions is usually the most extreme of all of the patterns.

Despite the typically severe reversals, the focus of the pattern's completion should examine the 1.618 XA projection. In most cases, it is best to wait for the 1.618 to be tested. However, the convergence of the BC projection should serve as the minimum requirement for the pattern to be considered complete. The most distinct Crab structures will typically possess a precise range of the XA and BC projections. Again, the AB=CD pattern, whether the equivalent or alternate calculation, should complement this area, but it is not a significant consideration in the PRZ.

Crab pattern elements:

- **B point that is a 0.618 retracement of XA or less.**
- **Extreme BC projection that is typically a 2.618, 3.14, or 3.618.**
- **Alternate 1.27 or 1.618 AB=CD pattern required.**
- **1.618 XA projection as the defining limit with the structure.**
- **C point with range between 0.382 and 0.886.**

It is important to understand that the Crab is a unique 5-point corrective structure. Although the pattern's dependence on the 1.618 XA projection to define the completion area is critical, it is not the only element in the structure. Essentially, the Crab is more than just a 1.618 extension. As I discussed previously regarding the importance of pattern differentiation, the specification of all points within the Crab is essential to find the most valid structures. Furthermore, this specification relates to all patterns, especially extension patterns.

I would like to take a moment to discuss the difference between retracement and extension patterns. Retracement patterns, like the Bat or the Gartley, are 5-point corrective structures that retest a critical high or low point, which is the initial point (X). In combination with some type of AB=CD structure, the completion of the pattern possesses a defined range of harmonic numbers—the PRZ.

These numbers serve as the pivot area relative to the initial starting point (X) for the anticipated reversal. Essentially, if the price action exceeds the initial starting point (X), the pattern is considered violated and the stop loss is executed. Therefore, the retracement patterns possess more clearly defined parameters. In particular, the initial point (X) is the determining level. In comparison, extension patterns like the Crab do not possess significant relative validation levels. The initial point (X) is a less significant point in the extension structure than a retracement pattern. Furthermore, the stop loss consideration is typically more subjective, and the treatment of the price action in the PRZ must be handled differently.

The determination of the validity of extension patterns may require more risk in the actual trade execution of the setup than most retracement situations. Although these strategies will be covered extensively in Chapter 11, "The Harmonic Trade Management System," it is important to realize the difference between these two types of patterns.

The Bullish Crab Pattern

The Bullish Crab pattern possesses a distinct structure with an extended final leg (see Figure 7.1). It is common for price action to become extreme as the pattern approaches its completion point. Again, it is best to wait for the 1.618 XA extension to be tested, but the BC projection should be a significant consideration and a minimum price level within the PRZ. In addition, the Alternate 1.27 or 1.618 AB=CD should complement this area.

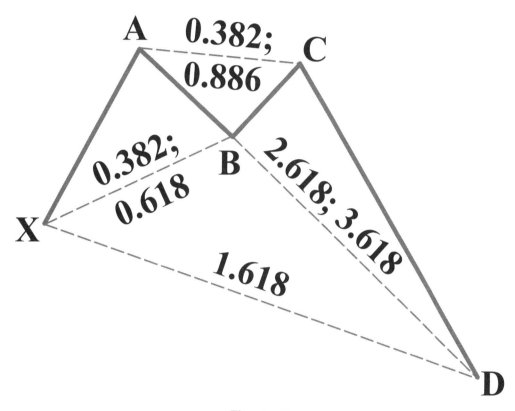

Figure 7.1

Apple (AAPL): 15-Minute

Figure 7.2 is an example of an intra-day Bullish Crab in Apple which possessed a distinct 1.618 projection with a 3.14 BC projection that completed in the same area. The completion of the Crab included an Alternate 1.618 AB=CD pattern that defined the top range of the PRZ. Although AB=CD pattern consideration is less important in the Crab pattern, it is still utilized with the other more significant numbers—the 1.618 XA projection and the 3.14 BC projection. For Apple, the Bullish Crab clearly defined the 162 level as important intra-day support.

Figure 7.2

This intra-day chart of Apple also reveals the typical extreme price action that can occur as the pattern nears completion. The sharp sell-off into the PRZ reflects the nature of both the 1.618 XA leg and the smaller yet more extended BC leg. These projections typically serve as the most important support levels at the completion of the pattern. In this example of Apple, the stock sank sharply before stabilizing in the PRZ. Shortly after all of the numbers in the zone were tested, the price action reversed decisively and marked a critical intra-day turning point. Figure 7.3 of the price action in the PRZ shows the ideal reversal that occurred after all of the harmonic numbers were tested.

The tight convergence of the 1.618 XA and the 3.14 BC projection just above 162 was clearly the defining limit of the PRZ. Sometimes, the Alternate AB=CD pattern will complement the other two more significant numbers in the PRZ. In the case of Apple, the structure was quite distinct and possessed a substantial 1.618 XA extension. This chart of the price action in the Potential Reversal Zone also shows an ideal turnaround in the stock immediately after all of the numbers were tested. In intra-day situations like these, valid reversals will possess price action that responds dramatically to precise areas of harmonic support.

Figure 7.3

General Electric (GE): 60-Minute

This 60-minute chart of General Electric shows another distinct intra-day Bullish Crab that reversed immediately after testing the entire PRZ (see Figure 7.4).

Figure 7.4

Although the pattern possessed the required alignment of Fibonacci ratios to validate the structure, the Alternate 1.618 AB=CD projection was not as close to the most important number in the PRZ—the 1.618 XA leg. The XA leg defined the lower range of the PRZ at 10.75, while the BC projection complemented this area precisely. Clearly, the stock stabilized after testing the entire zone and quickly confirmed the reversal, as the upside continuation decisively rallied from the harmonic support. Again, the XA and BC legs were the defining limit of the pattern while the AB=CD consideration merely complemented the harmonic support. The following chart of the price action in the PRZ shows how the stock stabilized at the convergence of the 1.618 XA and 2.618 BC projections (see Figure 7.5). The reversal completed within a few days after the initial test of the harmonic support.

Figure 7.5

Again, it is important to note that the Crab pattern is less reliant on the three calculations that typically define a PRZ. Although the Alternate AB=CD is merely complementary in this Crab, the support defined by the PRZ is as accurate and effective as any pattern.

Standard and Poor's 500 September Mini-Contract (ES_U3): 10-Minute

The September 2003 ES Mini-contract formed a distinct Bullish Crab on this 10-minute chart (see Figure 7.6). The pattern possessed nice symmetry with an ideal alignment of harmonic numbers that defined a PRZ at the 1000 level. The convergence of the 1.618 XA and the 3.14 BC projections at the same level defined an ideal PRZ for the Crab pattern.

Figure 7.6

This setup was actually featured in my advisory service that I previously provided on my website, HarmonicTrader.com. Although the pattern in the ES completed during the overnight session, it still represented a valid trading opportunity. I outlined the situation in this day's Mini-Room post on my website, HarmonicTrader.com. On July 15, 2003, in the pre-market report, I wrote:

"For today's immediate action, the ES is up 7 in the pre-market. The ES reversed from this Bullish Crab in the overnight session. This complements the 1000 level and is now critical short-term support.

The open is critical for today's trend. I would wait for the ES to pull back slightly on (another) attempt to refill today's upside gap. I would watch for an early morning reversal...as an area to get long for an attempt at new short-term highs."

(HarmonicTrader.com, July 15, 2003, http://www.harmonictrader.com/ members/harmonic/home/miniroom071503.htm)

Although the price action did not offer a retest to get long in the PRZ, this set-up clearly identified the critical intra-day support in the ES. Despite the extreme sell-off into the PRZ, the ES stabilized after testing all of the numbers in the zone.

It is important to note that the initial point (X) utilized an "intermediate point" to begin the pattern. The intermediate point, although not the clear low from the prior's day action, was defined well enough to establish the appropriate alignment of Fibonacci numbers in the structure. This structure illustrates the importance of the relative alignment of ratios to define a pattern. The formation of various patterns do not have to initiate from an absolute low or high. Although XA legs that are well defined typically originate from an extreme price level, the symmetry and validity of a particular pattern are more dependent upon the segments that comprise each structure. In this example of the ES, both the XA and BC legs were distinct and effectively outlined the pattern's completion, despite originating from an intermediate support point from the prior day.

Another consideration of this setup is the psychological price level that coincided with the projected harmonic support. It is important to respect obvious "psychological" price levels that occur at the completion of harmonic patterns. Price levels such as 50, 100, or 1000 can frequently complement areas of harmonic support or resistance. In this case, the ES was challenging the all-important 1000 level.

These situations are common and underscore the importance of Fibonacci alignments to define potential harmonic structures. In fact, the various alignments of ratios that define structures as valid patterns is one of the fundamental principles that separates Harmonic Trading from all other Fibonacci-related methodologies. Furthermore, in my research of the past ten years, the importance of ratio alignments has become more significant in validating price structures as harmonic patterns.

On a side note, this intra-day chart example included a pattern that completed during the overnight session. In recent years with the advent of 24-hour trading, the debate of which data to use has become increasingly significant. Some have argued that only the regular session (9:30 a.m.–4:00 p.m. EST) should be utilized. However, the surge in pre- and post-market action, especially in futures contracts such as the Standard and Poor's 500 (SPX) or its "mini-me" sibling the ES, necessitates the inclusion of all trading action. The example of the ES is a clear case of this technical phenomenon.

Although this situation can be difficult, a clear pattern that completes in the after-market while most are sleeping can result in missed opportunities. Simply stated, trades—even the best harmonic patterns—will be missed. Despite the inevitable frustration that may be associated with these episodes, the pattern did clearly outline the short-term support and distinct opportunity to get long the ES.

The Bearish Crab Pattern

The Bearish Crab pattern is a precise structure with a PRZ consisting of three numbers, the 1.618 XA retracement, the Alternate AB=CD, and an extreme BC projection (see Figure 7.7).

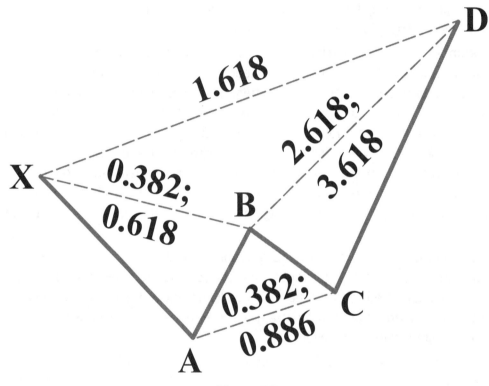

Figure 7.7

The convergence of the XA and BC projections define the top range of the Potential Reversal Zone. The 1.27 or the 1.618 Alternate AB=CD pattern typically complements the other numbers at the pattern's completion point. As was previously mentioned, the AB=CD pattern is not as critical in the PRZ for the Crab as other patterns. At a minimum, the XA must be tested before the reversal can be considered complete and the pattern a valid set-up. Although price action may slightly exceed the 1.618 XA leg on the initial test of the PRZ, the completion point in valid Crab patterns will mark the precise turning point for the reversal.

Qualcomm (QCOM): 60-Minute

This intra-day Bearish Crab shows a distinct pattern with a convergence of the 1.618 XA and the 2.618 BC projections and the Alternate 1.618 AB=CD completion defining a tight zone to short the stock in the 42.75–43.70 range (see Figure 7.8).

Figure 7.8

After opening slightly above the top range of the PRZ, the stock stalled at the harmonic resistance and quickly declined within a short time after testing the entire range of harmonic resistance. The following chart of the price action in the Potential Reversal Zone (PRZ) shows the ideal reversal at the numbers (see Figure 7.9). Although QCOM opened above the zone, the stock's inability to continue the upside momentum is typically a sign of a reversal in progress. In this case, the gap up on the open failed miserably in a distinct Bearish Crab PRZ.

Figure 7.9

This type of price action is common in the PRZ for the Crab pattern and exemplifies the extreme price action that can be found in valid reversals. The immediate price action following the test of all the numbers at the pattern's completion point is one of the primary considerations in the validity of the setup. In this case, the clear failure of the rally in the PRZ marked the reversal.

Light Sweet Crude Continuous Contract (CL_#F): 15-Minute

This intra-day chart of the continuous contract of Light Sweet Crude (CL_#F) exhibits the typical extreme price action that can occur as the pattern nears completion (see Figure 7.10). The sharp rally into the PRZ reflects the extreme inherent nature that both the 1.618 XA leg and the smaller yet more extended BC leg possess. Furthermore, these projections typically serve as the most important support levels at the completion of the pattern. In this example of Crude Oil, the price action quickly tested the completion of the pattern and reversed quickly from this PRZ.

Figure 7.10

The following chart shows the price action at the completion of the pattern. The rally stalled right at the numbers and reversed exactly at the top end of the intraday harmonic resistance. The distinct change in the nature of the preceding uptrend was the overwhelming sign that the reversal was valid. The execution of the short should have focused on the price action immediately following the completion of the Crab pattern, as the price action provided immediate signs of a valid reversal.

Figure 7.11

It is important to remember that the Crab PRZ is primarily defined by only the XA and BC projections. In most instances, the Alternate AB=CD pattern does not complete in the vicinity of these other two calculations. Although the AB=CD pattern completion sometimes complements the other numbers more closely, the setup is primarily defined by the 1.618 XA projection.

NASDAQ 100 December 2003 Mini-Contract (NQ_Z3): 5-Minute

Incredible structure! The example of the December 2003 NASDAQ 100 Mini-contract exemplified all the ideal elements of a Bearish Crab (see Figure 7.12). The tight convergence of the 1.618 XA leg and the BC projection yielded an exact reversal and outlined a perfect situation and a distinct trading opportunity to get short at the 1420 level.

Figure 7.12

I mentioned this previously, but I believe it is important to emphasize the advantage of utilizing all trading data available, especially in futures markets to analyze potential harmonic patterns. The NQ formed this pattern over the course of two days of trading, including an overnight and pre-market session. This 5-minute chart is an excellent intra-day example that formed the pattern utilizing all trading action over the course of a continuous 30-hour period.

The Deep Crab Pattern

The Deep Crab pattern evolved from two patterns—invalid Bat patterns and a specific type of Crab pattern—that I developed as a further refinement of the basic structure. The Deep Crab is similar to the original Crab pattern, as it is a 5-point extension structure that utilizes exclusively a 1.618 XA projection for the defining level in the Potential Reversal Zone (PRZ). The difference can be found at the B point which must be an 0.886 retracement. In fact, the Deep Crab pattern usually possesses a B point that is beyond the 0.886 level but it does not violate the initial point (X). The 0.886 B point requirement is special to the Deep Crab. When the structure is in the midst of completing the CD leg, the violation of the B point AND the X point typically creates a situation of severe price action. In essence, the price action is violating two important prior support or resistance points. When this happens, the result is frequently a sharp move that quickly extends to the 1.618 XA projection.

Another difference in the Deep Crab pattern is the AB=CD structure. The AB=CD pattern is a more important consideration in the Deep Crab, although the structure typically possesses the 1.27AB=CD alternate variation. However, it is common for these structures to possess equivalent AB=CD patterns in certain circumstances. In a normal Crab, the "shallow" B point retracement of a 0.618 or less creates an elongated CD leg, which typically sets up an Alternate 1.618 AB=CD pattern. However, the Deep Crab's alignment of Fibonacci ratios, especially the 0.886 B point, creates a structure with an alignment that often possesses significant AB=CD patterns.

The treatment of the BC projection is slightly different in the Deep Crab, as well. The BC projection is usually less extreme than the regular structure. Specifically, the BC projection possesses a minimum 2.24 measurement, but the variations can include extensions as large as a 3.618. It depends upon the AB=CD completion that best fits the 1.618 XA projection.

Similar to the regular Crab pattern, the 1.618 XA leg is the defining Fibonacci measurement in the pattern. The 1.618 projection underscores the extreme nature of the pattern, and it is typical for price action to be volatile and reverse sharply from these PRZ.

Although these structures possess similar elements, their differentiated alignments, especially their respective B point ratios, serve to differentiate these as unique harmonic patterns. In fact, the Deep Crab is a different pattern than both the regular version of the Crab and the Butterfly. Such precise pattern specification is one of the fundamental principles that separate Harmonic Trading from all other pattern recognition methodologies. Although these three structures appear similar, their respective Fibonacci alignments clearly differentiate them as distinct patterns.

The Deep Bullish Crab Pattern

The Deep Bullish Crab is a distinct structure that is defined by the 0.886 B point retracement of the XA leg (see Figure 7.13). The 1.618 XA leg should be the lowest point in the PRZ and the defining limit in the completion of the pattern. The pattern usually possesses some type of Alternate Bullish AB=CD that requires either a 1.27 or 1.618 calculation.

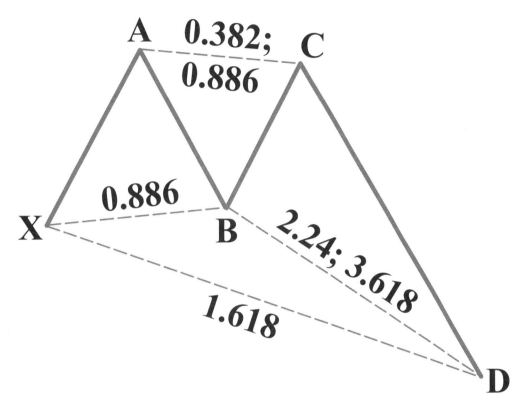

Figure 7.13

NASDAQ 100 December 2003 Mini-Contract (NQ_Z3): 15-Minute

This Deep Bullish Crab formed on the 15-minute chart of the NQ (see Figure 7.14). This pattern exemplifies a distinct Deep Crab structure, and it possessed three numbers, the 1.618 XA projection, a 1.27AB=CD, and a 3.14 BC projection, that converged just above 1427.

Figure 7.14

Such an exact alignment of numbers in the PRZ frequently offers a sizeable initial reaction at a minimum. In this case, the NQ rallied exactly from the pattern's completion.

The chart in Figure 7.15 of the price action in the PRZ shows an ideal reversal exactly at the harmonic numbers. This setup is a great case of a sharp reversal that can occur in Crab patterns. Again, it is common for Crab patterns—Deep or regular—to experience reversals that possess extreme price action in the PRZ.

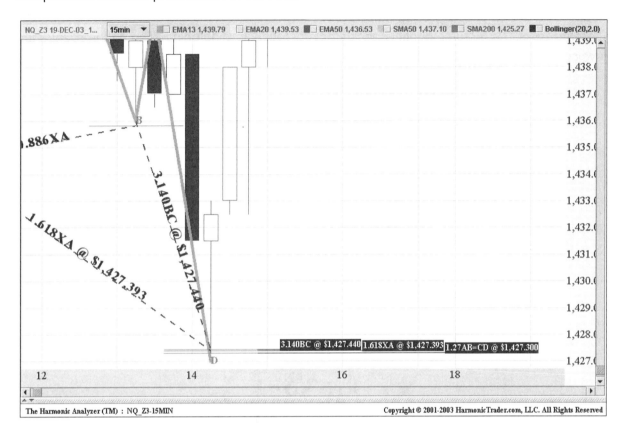

Figure 7.15

It is important to note that such a convergence of Fibonacci calculations grouped this closely together must be regarded as an extremely harmonic area. This is an extraordinary example where three numbers completed within 1 tick (1/2 point), providing an excellent intra-day setup.

The Deep Bearish Crab Pattern

The Deep Bearish Crab pattern utilizes a 1.618 XA projection exclusively for the defining level in the PRZ (see Figure 7.16). The 0.886 retracement at the B point validates the structure as "deep" in nature. Essentially, this pattern possesses multiple extensions that combined with an Alternate AB=CD structure, identify considerable potential turning points. The pattern frequently develops after a trend has been established in patterns with an extreme BC projection.

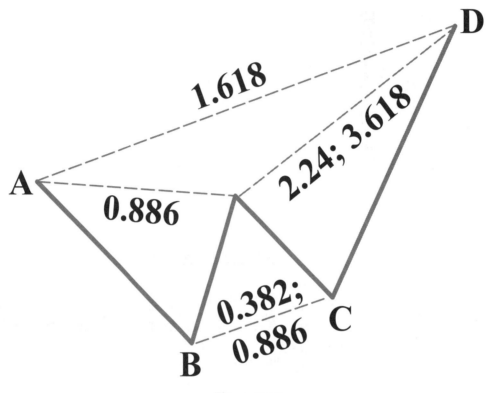

Figure 7.16

Anadarko Petroleum (APC): Daily

Anadarko Petroleum formed this distinct Deep Bearish Crab that possessed three numbers defining a tight 30-cent PRZ (see Figure 7.17). This is remarkable due to the fact that the pattern comprises nearly a 30 points range. The 1.618 XA projection, the Alternate 1.27 AB=CD pattern, and the 2.24 BC projection converged in the same area at $78.80.

Figure 7.17

The price action stalled immediately after testing the entire PRZ and the stock reversed considerably soon after. Although the price action rallied sharply as it approached the completion of the pattern, the obvious stalling that occurred followed by the decisive downside continuation were the definitive technical signs of a valid reversal. The price action reversed quickly after slightly exceeding the top range of the PRZ and briefly tested the psychological $80 level. The chart in Figure 7.18 of the Potential Reversal Zone clearly shows the price action failing to continue to rally above the harmonic resistance. Furthermore, the psychological $80 level added to the resistance of the pattern, as the stock dropped sharply within several days of testing the entire PRZ.

Figure 7.18

The Perfect Crab Pattern

The Crab pattern is defined by a 0.618 B point retracement, a 1.618 XA projection, and a 3.14 BC projection. Utilizing two extremely harmonic measures, 1.618 (Phi) and 3.14 (Pi), the perfect Crab represents a unique structure and an incredibly precise pattern.

> **1. Precise 0.618 B point retracement of the XA leg.**
>
> **2. 3.14 BC projection.**
>
> **3. 1.618 AB=CD.**
>
> **4. C point within a 50–61.8% range.**

The Perfect Bullish Crab Pattern

The perfect Bullish Crab pattern in Figure 7.19 is a distinct structure that possesses a precise alignment of 0.618 B point retracement, a 1.618 XA projection, an Alternate 1.618 AB=CD, and a 3.14 BC projection.

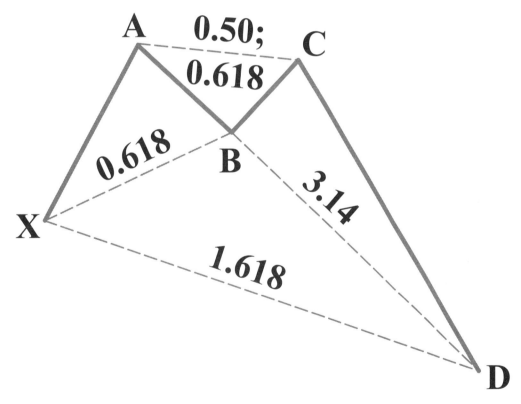

Figure 7.19

Home Depot (HD): 15-Minute

This Perfect Crab in Home Depot (HD) exemplifies the proper alignment of Fibonacci ratios required to validate the structure (see Figure 7.20). The pattern is defined by a precise 0.618 B point retracement of the XA leg. The 1.618 XA projection is the lowest point in the PRZ, and the Alternate 1.618 AB=CD with the 3.14 BC projection contributed to the harmonic support in the 32.50–32.75 range.

Figure 7.20

The chart in Figure 7.21 of the price action in the PRZ shows an ideal reversal after the 1.618 XA projection was tested. This is another example of a sharp price action as the stock traded into the PRZ. Home Depot reversed almost exactly after hitting the 1.618 XA projection at 32.55.

Figure 7.21

Perfect Crab patterns such as these frequently experience sharp and dramatic price action at their completion points. The stock reversed immediately after testing the most important number in the setup—the 1.618 XA. Despite the sharp intra-day decline, the pattern clearly defined the short-term support.

The Perfect Bearish Crab Pattern

The perfect Bearish Crab is a distinct 5-point extension structure that combines the particularly harmonic ratios of the 1.618 at the XA leg and the 3.14 at the BC leg (see Figure 7.22). This unique alignment frequently defines remarkable trading opportunities and incredibly precise resistance zones.

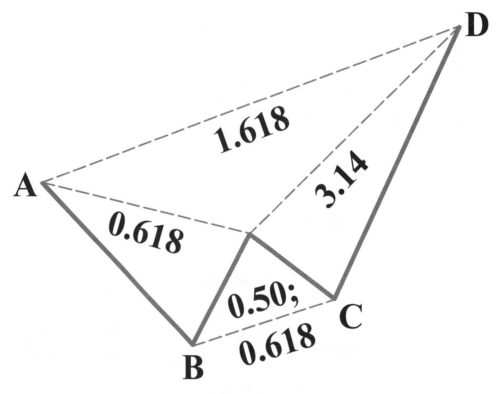

Figure 7.22

Nokia (NOK): 5-Minute

Nokia formed this Perfect Bullish Crab on the following 5-minute chart (see Figure 7.23). This pattern exemplifies the proper alignment of Fibonacci ratios required to validate the setup. The precise 0.618 B point retracement of the XA leg is the defining element that establishes the structure.

Figure 7.23

The 1.618 XA projection defined the top range of the PRZ and the Alternate 1.618 AB=CD with the 3.14 BC projection complemented the harmonic resistance in the 17.20 area.

This is another example of a typical extreme price move into the PRZ for a Crab pattern. Although the stock rallied sharply, as it gapped up on the open, into the harmonic resistance, the stock stalled immediately and rolled over, completing an ideal reversal.

The Crab Pattern Summary

Although the structural variations of the Crab may seem to define the same pattern, the alignment of Fibonacci ratios clearly differentiates each type as a unique situation. The Crab typically defines extreme overbought and oversold situations, as the 1.618 XA leg is the most important Fibonacci measurement of the pattern and it represents the most critical number in the Potential Reversal Zone (PRZ).

Unlike the other patterns within the Harmonic Trading approach, the AB=CD is not as critical at the completion point. Although it is important to differentiate the AB=CD possibilities for each variation, the Alternate 1.618 AB=CD pattern is the preferred structure in most Crab patterns. However, the 1.27 AB=CD pattern is typically found in the original version, while it is not unusual for the Deep Crab to possess an equivalent AB=CD.

The extreme BC projection—usually a 2.618, 3.14, or 3.618 extension—underscores the nature of this structure. Although the Deep Crab permits a wider range of BC possibilities, this projection should converge closely with the 1.618 XA.

1. **Precise 0.618 B point retracement or less of the XA leg. (.382 and 0.50 are common B points in the structure.)**
2. **Extreme 2.618, 3.14 or 3.618BC projection. (Sometimes 2.24 BC projections form in the structure.)**
3. **Minimum AB=CD completion. Alternate 1.27 AB=CD or 1.618 AB=CD patterns are most common.**
4. **C point retracement can vary between a 0.382 to an 0.886.**
5. **This is an extreme pattern!**

The volatile nature of this pattern must be emphasized. Reversals from these PRZs can be sharp and possess extreme price action. The Crab is a distinctive pattern and possesses unique qualities that identify remarkable harmonic opportunities. The differentiation of this pattern is critical to define each variation.

From a harmonic perspective, valid Crab structures identify extreme oversold or overbought conditions. These patterns usually offer some type of reaction on the initial test of the Potential Reversal Zone. The price action frequently responds to extreme Fibonacci projection combinations within the Crab pattern of the 1.618 XA leg and the 2.618 or greater BC leg. The Crab is an incredibly accurate and consistently effective pattern within the Harmonic Trading arsenal to identify critical turning points in the markets.

Chapter 8

The Ideal Butterfly Pattern

Bryce Gilmore discovered the structure of the Butterfly pattern in his *Wave Trader* software program. Although his interpretation of the structure encompasses a multitude of Fibonacci combinations, I believe the specification of each point within the structure is essential to be able to successfully trade the pattern. As the example of the Crab pattern demonstrated, the alignment of pattern points is critical. The Butterfly pattern is no different, as specific alignments within this 5-point extension structure are the key to finding the best opportunities.

In my experience, I believe an *ideal* Butterfly pattern requires a specific alignment of Fibonacci measurements at each point within the structure. Most important, a mandatory 0.786 retracement of the XA leg as the B point is the defining element of an ideal Butterfly pattern, and it acts as the primary measuring point to define a specific Potential Reversal Zone (PRZ).

In many ways, the ideal Butterfly pattern is like the Gartley pattern because it requires a specific B point retracement and possesses a tighter array of Fibonacci ratios within the structure. Specifically, the Butterfly incorporates a 1.27 XA projection with a "tame" BC projection, which is usually only a 1.618. In addition, the Butterfly usually possesses an equivalent AB=CD pattern or an Alternate 1.27 AB=CD pattern. Although the equivalent AB=CD is a minimum requirement, valid Butterfly structures rarely exceed the Alternate 1.27 AB=CD completion point.

The Crab Pattern Versus the Butterfly Pattern

The difference between a Crab and a Butterfly is vast. Although these price structures appear similar since they represent two types of extension patterns, their measurements clearly differentiate their characteristics. The Crab utilizes a 1.618 XA projection, while the *ideal* Butterfly pattern utilizes a 1.27 XA projection exclusively. Essentially, the Crab is a reactionary pattern that attempts to define extreme oversold and overbought situations. An ideal Butterfly pattern is differentiated by a 0.786 retracement at the B point. Utilizing this alignment for an ideal Butterfly pattern can eliminate many invalid imposters—those price structures "posing" as potential valid patterns that are common failures.

The AB=CD pattern is another critical element for an ideal Butterfly pattern to be a valid signal. It is important to note that the AB=CD pattern frequently will possess an alternate structure that is typically 1.27 of the AB leg. Although this is an important requirement for a valid trade signal, the most critical number in the ideal Butterfly pattern is the 1.27 XA leg. The XA calculation is usually complemented by a 1.618, 2.00, or 2.24 BC projection. Although the 2.618 is sometimes utilized to complement a PRZ, the smaller BC projections work the best with the 1.27 XA primary price leg. In essence, the BC projection should complete in a "compact" area with the 1.27 XA leg. These numbers create a specific PRZ that can yield powerful reversals, especially when the pattern is in all-time (new highs/new lows) price levels. The ideal Butterfly works well in new high/low territory because valid patterns frequently represent critical 5-point reversal structures that frequently trigger the end of the predominant trend. The following illustrations and examples demonstrate these concepts.

Ideal Butterfly pattern elements:

- **Precise 78.6% B point retracement of XA leg.**
- **BC projection must be at least a 1.618.**
- **Equivalent AB=CD pattern is minimum requirement, but the Alternate 1.27 AB=CD is the most common.**
- **1.27 XA projection most critical number in the Potential Reversal Zone (PRZ).**
- **No 1.618 XA projection.**
- **C point within range of 0.382–0.886 retracement.**

The Bullish Butterfly Pattern

Beginning with a precise 0.786 B point retracement, the Bullish Butterfly (see Figure 8.1) encompasses a minimum AB=CD pattern with the 1.27 XA and the 1.618 BC projections as mandatory requirements to define the Potential Reversal Zone (PRZ).

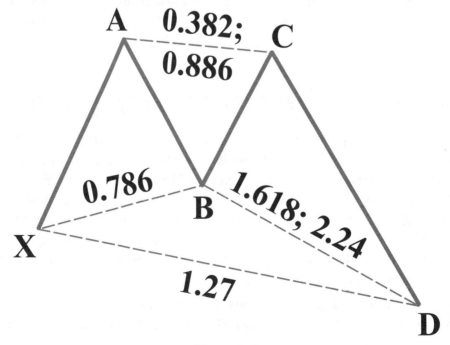

Figure 8.1

Standard and Poor's 500 Tracking Stock (SPY): Daily

In Figure 8.2, the SPY formed this ideal Butterfly pattern that exemplified the proper alignment of Fibonacci ratios required to validate the structure. The 0.786 B point retracement of the XA leg is the defining element in this example that establishes the structure. The 1.27 XA projection defined the lower range of the PRZ, while the Alternate 1.27 AB=CD and the 1.618 BC projection contributed to the harmonic support just under the $70 level.

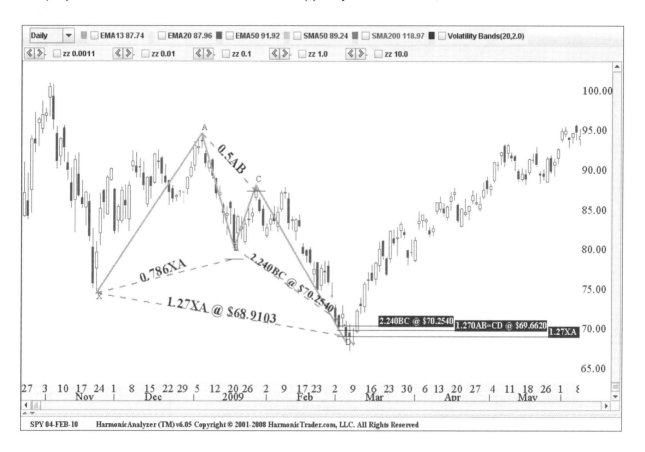

Figure 8.2

This was a substantial structural signal, as it was the defining pattern that marked the 2009 bear market low. The following chart of the price action in the PRZ shows an ideal reversal after all the numbers were tested (see Figure 8.3). After a steady decline, the SPY stabilized just below the projected harmonic support.

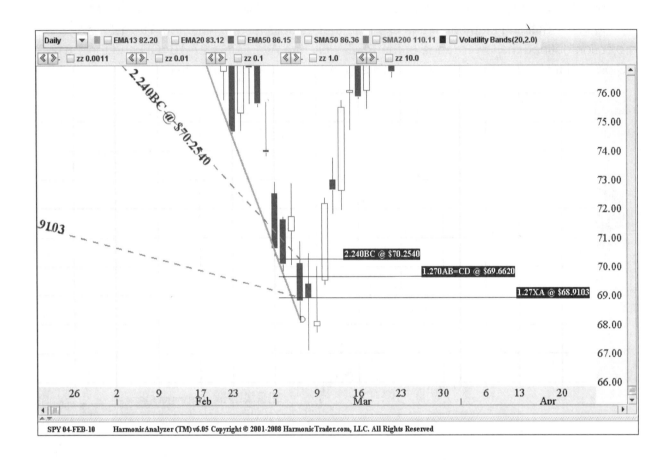

Figure 8.3

This example possessed a dramatic reversal. On the day the price action tested all of the numbers in the PRZ, the downtrend started to stabilize. The following two days challenged the PRZ. After the reversal was complete, the price action rallied convincingly, as it closed above harmonic support. Although the price action required a few more days to stabilize, the completion of the pattern clearly marked a critical low for the SPY.

American Express
(AXP): 60-Minute

This Bullish Butterfly on the 60-minute chart of American Express is an excellent example of a precise 0.786 B point retracement that defined the structure (see Figure 8.4). The 1.618 BC projection and the Alternate 1.618 AB=CD complemented the harmonic support at the $32 level.

Figure 8.4

The pattern formed on this 60-minute chart over the course of several sessions and signaled a resumption of the predominant uptrend. After a week of consolidation, the distinct pattern defined critical support in a narrow ten-cent range in the $32 area. The price action rallied immediately following the completion of the pattern.

Such a close congregation of numbers in the PRZ is another sign of a significant harmonic setup. Furthermore, the pattern's structure possessed ideal symmetry and reversed convincingly after the initial PRZ test (see Figure 8.5). All of these factors were solid indicators that signaled a potential reversal. Although such setups do not guarantee a successful reversal, these are the traits that define the best opportunities.

Figure 8.5

It is important to note that the Butterfly is similar to the Gartley because the B point is so critical in validating the structure as a harmonic pattern. For a Butterfly, the B point must possess a 78.6% retracement. As this enlarged chart of AXP illustrates, the precise B point established the proper alignment of ratios, resulting in a defined completion area for the pattern. Although the ideal conditions do not occur in every situation, these guidelines serve to define the clearest opportunities and differentiate various structures as precisely as possible.

Petrobras (PBR): Daily 60-Minute

This daily chart of Petrobras exemplifies the ideal structure that valid Bullish Butterfly patterns should possess (see Figure 8.6). The setup possessed an ideal alignment of Fibonacci ratios to validate the structure, including an exact 0.786 B point retracement of the XA leg.

Figure 8.6

The 1.27 XA leg defined the lower range of the PRZ at 82.75, while the 1.618 BC projection and the 1.27 AB=CD pattern complemented this area at 84.06 and 83.45, respectively. The price action was able to stabilize on the day the stock tested all of the numbers in the PRZ. In fact, the reversal was ideal, as the stock dropped sharply into the PRZ, hit the entire range of numbers, and closed above the harmonic support. Although this was a dramatic reversal, the Bullish Butterfly clearly defined the area for a critical turning point in the trend of the stock. Petrobras stabilized above the PRZ and accelerated to the upside several days later to confirm the pattern completion (see Figure 8.7).

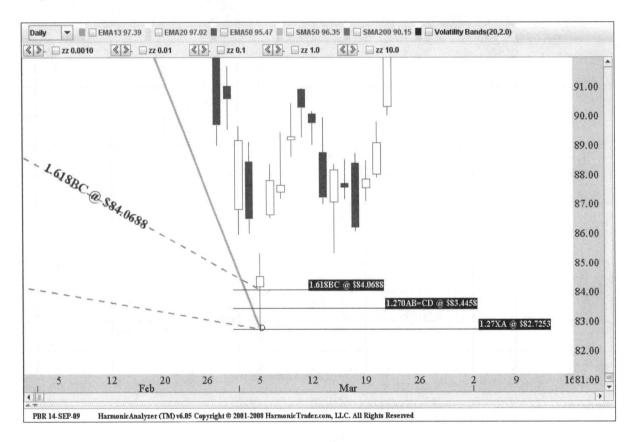

Figure 8.7

Although the price action declined sharply as it entered the PRZ, the pattern completion point put a floor under the stock. The fact that the stock was able to close above the top range of the harmonic support was another indication of a valid reversal in the works.

Standard and Poor's 500 Mini-Contract (September 2009) (ES_U9): 60-Minute

The Bullish Butterfly on the 60-minute chart of the Standard and Poor's 500 September 2009 Mini-Contract (see Figure 8.8) is another excellent example of a precise 0.786 B point retracement that defined the structure. The 2.0 BC projection and the AB=CD pattern complemented the harmonic support at the 977 level.

Figure 8.8

This distinct pattern materialized in ideal fashion on this 60-minute chart over the course of several sessions. Although the price action required two complete tests of the PRZ as it consolidated following a steep three-day decline, the completion area for the setup defined critical support just under the 980 level and pinpointed the optimal entry for the long position.

The Bearish Butterfly Pattern

The ideal Bearish Butterfly structure is defined by a precise 0.786 B point retracement of the XA leg (see Figure 8.9). The setup requires an AB=CD pattern that should converge with the 1.27 XA and the 1.618 BC projections as minimum conditions to define the PRZ.

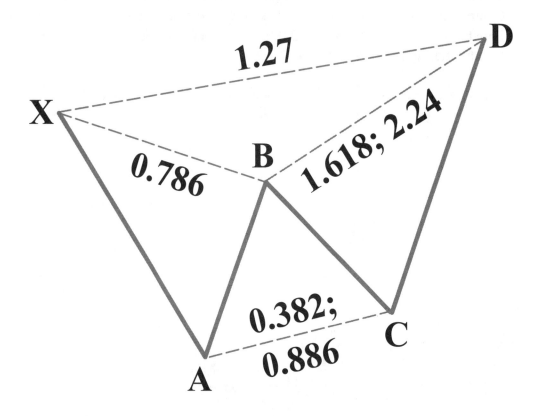

Figure 8.9

Citigroup (C): Weekly

The weekly chart of Citigroup (see Figure 8.10) was the fateful long-term pattern that marked the top in the stock before its remarkable demise. This long-term pattern formed over the course of four years before reversing dramatically.

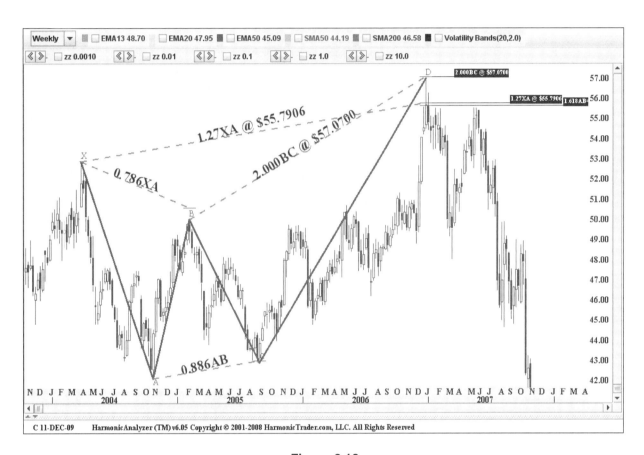

Figure 8.10

The Butterfly possessed the ideal elements for a valid structure, including a precise B point retracement at the 0.786 of the XA leg. The Alternate 1.27 AB=CD complemented the 1.27 XA projection that clearly defined harmonic resistance just above the $55 level. In fact, these two extensions overlapped each other at 55.80, defining the optimal entry for the trade. Figure 8.11 of the price action in the Potential Reversal Zone (PRZ) shows an ideal reversal the week after the entire range was tested. The price action stalled the following price bar after the completion of the pattern and the stock declined sharply immediately after the initial reaction. In fact, the weekly price bar that initially tested the entire range of numbers closed below the PRZ. In addition, the subsequent weekly price bars nominally retested the PRZ but repeatedly closed below the harmonic resistance. Such price action is indicative of a valid reversal and represents one of the clear signs of a potential change in trend.

Figure 8.11

This example of Citigroup emphasizes the ability of harmonic patterns to identify critical turning points in the financial markets on any timeframe. In this case, the long-term nature of the setup was quite significant. Although the complete collapse of the stock could not have been predicted based upon the Butterfly pattern alone, the weekly price action clearly indicated major resistance that was to be regarded. At a minimum, the setup indicated a substantial selling opportunity. As the stock rolled over the next several months, the severity of the decline became evident.

Swiss Franc
(CHF_A0-FX): 60-Minute

The next example of a Bearish Butterfly in the Swiss Franc shows another excellent harmonic pattern in the currency markets (see Figure 8.12). The 60-minute chart possessed a distinct pattern that clearly defined the critical resistance. The pattern formed the required Fibonacci alignment to validate the Butterfly structure and the price action rolled over nicely after testing the entire PRZ. The pattern marked an important reversal of the predominant intra-day trend.

Figure 8.12

Although the CD was somewhat extended, the structure was quite distinct with a tight range of numbers to define the completion of the pattern. The reversal occurred shortly after testing the entire range of harmonic resistance.

Figure 8.13 of the price action in the Potential Reversal Zone shows an ideal reversal after the entire range was tested. The Swiss Franc stalled in an ideal fashion immediately following the completion of the pattern.

Figure 8.13

The last two examples exhibited similar reversals on two different timeframes. The weekly Butterfly in Citigroup and the 60-minute setup in the Swiss Franc possessed almost exactly the same pattern alignments. The nature of each reversal was similar, despite the difference of the respective timeframes. These examples underscore the uniformity in the application of the Harmonic Trading principles, regardless of the timeframe and market being analyzed. Each situation should be handled in similar fashion while always being mindful of the respective timeframe that is being analyzed.

The Perfect Butterfly Pattern

The Perfect Butterfly pattern is defined by a B point retracement that an exact 78.6% of the XA leg to set up the ideal alignment of Fibonacci ratios. Another distinctive aspect of the Perfect Butterfly structure is a precise 1.618 BC leg that complements completion of the 1.27 XA leg. Although the ideal Butterfly alignment permits some variation of the BC projection—up to a 2.24—the perfect structure possesses only a 1.618 BC. Although the ideal Butterfly alignment permits either AB=CD type, only the Alternate pattern 1.27 AB=CD is valid for the perfect pattern.

> 1. **Exact 0.786 B point retracement of the XA leg.**
> 2. **1.27 XA projection exclusively.**
> 3. **1.618 BC projection.**
> 4. **Alternate 1.27 AB=CD in the PRZ.**
> 5. **C point with range between 0.50 to 0.886 retracement.**

The Perfect Bullish Butterfly

The perfect Bullish Butterfly is a distinct 5-point extension structure that requires a specific alignment of Fibonacci numbers, including a 1.27 XA projection as the lowest limit in the PRZ (see Figure 8.14). The pattern must possess an Alternate 1.27 AB=CD pattern with a precise 1.618 BC projection, as well.

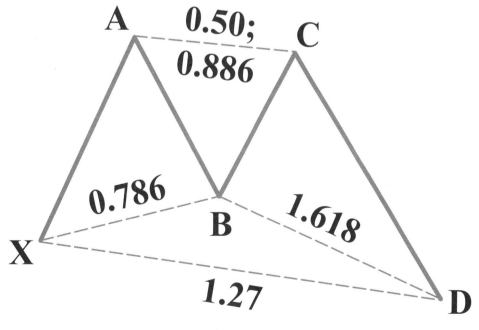

Figure 8.14

Japanese Yen
(JPY_A0-FX): 15-Minute

The Yen formed this perfect intra-day Bullish Butterfly that reversed exactly at the harmonic support (see Figure 8.15).

Figure 8.15

The structure possessed the required alignment of Fibonacci ratios to validate the perfect pattern. The 1.27 XA projection, the 1.618 BC projection and the Alternate 1.27 AB=CD converged in the 93.50 area to define the Potential Reversal Zone. The price action reversed exactly at the 1.27 XA leg and rallied sharply from this harmonic support.

   The chart in Figure 8.16 of the price action in the PRZ shows the exact reversal at the completion of the pattern. The Yen reversed immediately after testing the entire PRZ, and it possessed an ideal bullish continuation shortly after the completion of the pattern. Clearly, the price action stabilized as it initially tested the top range of the PRZ. After a brief consolidation period, the Yen reversed several hours later on a full retest of the support zone.

Figure 8.16

   The Yen reversed immediately after testing the entire PRZ and exploded to the upside. The dramatic bullish continuation exemplifies the potential of valid Perfect Butterfly structures. The perfect ratio alignment defines particularly reliable support zones and excellent trading opportunities, as each pattern completion is well defined and typically possesses ideal price action in the PRZ.

The Perfect Bearish Butterfly

The perfect Bearish Butterfly in Figure 8.17 is a distinct 5-point extension structure that utilizes the 1.27 XA projection as the highest limit in the PRZ. The pattern should possess an Alternate 1.27 AB=CD pattern with a 1.618 BC projection that complements the PRZ.

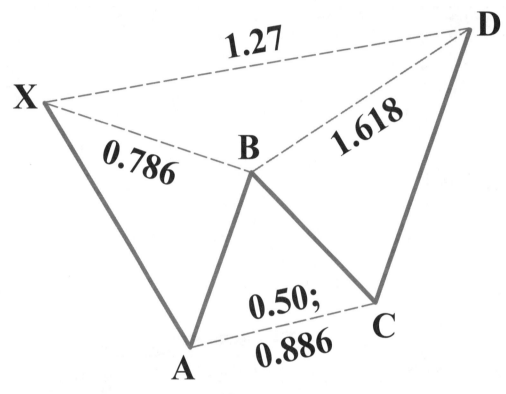

Figure 8.17

Standard and Poor's 500 Index ($SPX): 5-Minute

The S&P 500 Index formed this perfect Bearish Butterfly structure on the following 5-minute chart that possessed an ideal reversal at the completion of the pattern (see Figure 8.18).

Figure 8.18

On the following day after the stock tested all the numbers in the PRZ, the price action reversed sharply (see Figure 8.19). The resistance at the 1.27 XA projection defined the top range of the PRZ at 1005.48. Complementing this area, the Alternate 1.27 AB=CD pattern and the 2.0 BC projections defined the bottom and top of the PRZ, respectively.

Figure 8.19

Although the price action required a second intra-day test before triggering a more substantial reversal, the Perfect Bearish Butterfly clearly defined the critical short-term resistance for the index. This pattern exemplifies the ideal structure that perfect patterns should possess and illustrates their effectiveness to define excellent trading opportunities.

The Butterfly Pattern Summary

The Butterfly is a specific 5-point extension structure that possesses a distinct alignment of Fibonacci ratios to validate the pattern. The primary determining element of the pattern is a precise 0.786 B point retracement of the XA leg. The Butterfly utilizes only a 1.27 XA projection as the most critical number in the PRZ. Furthermore, the equivalent AB=CD pattern serves as a minimum requirement for the pattern's completion. But, the Alternate 1.27 AB=CD pattern is more common to the structure. The BC projection is another defining element of the pattern, as it must be at least a 1.618 extension. However, the BC projection is not as extreme in the Butterfly as it is in the Crab.

1. **Minimum AB=CD completion with Alternate 1.27 AB=CD pattern most common.**
2. **C point retracement can vary between a 0.382 to an 0.886, although 0.618 is preferred.**
3. **BC projection can vary from 1.13 to 3.618 and depends upon the C point retracement.**
4. **Alternate AB=CD patterns are common within the structure.**

The Butterfly is similar to the Gartley because it requires a specific alignment of Fibonacci ratios—especially a precise B point—to validate the structure. Although such a strict definition reduces the number of possible trading opportunities, this precision reduces those invalid situations that may appear similar but fail to yield consistently accurate setups.

Chapter 9

Trade Execution

After accurately identifying a potential trade opportunity, the actual price level for the execution must be determined. Several considerations must be assessed within a specific time period, as defined by the potential opportunity. Primarily, the validity of the pattern must be determined and the final action of whether or not to execute the trade or must be determined. Therefore, effective execution strategies can facilitate the process and optimize trading results.

Why Trading Tactics?

The key to successful trading requires thorough preparation. Investing the time to identify Harmonic Trading opportunities is only half of the battle. The other part that can be easily overlooked is the execution of the trade. Therefore, it is essential to create a set of rules in advance to resolve potential problems that may arise throughout the trading process.

Trading tactics are basic guidelines and strategies that optimize Harmonic Trading decisions. Such strategies provide rules for nearly every trading situation, attempting to maximize profits while limiting losses. Clearly, the Harmonic Trading techniques provide an accurate and effective means to identify critical turning points. However, each reversal is not the same. Hence, each monetary result—profit or loss—will differ based upon two critical factors:

1. **The market's reaction to the harmonic area.**
2. **Your response to the price action in the Potential Reversal Zone (PRZ).**

In this process, a variety of factors and potential trading decisions must be continually considered to maximize the result of the position. Since the same patterns yield different results, it can be difficult to try to "outguess the market" and know which setups will work. However, if a consistent set of rules is applied throughout the decision-making process, fewer mistakes will be made and more accurate assessments will improve the overall results of trade executions. In essence, the actions taken in accordance with these guidelines attempt to maximize profit while reducing risk.

What a Reversal Should Do

The critical factor in determining whether to execute a trade involves an understanding of how price action *should* act, after it has reversed from a harmonic area. Since a convergence of harmonic numbers defines a critical area for potential turning points, price action that begins to reverse from that area should clearly continue in that direction. In fact, in my research of harmonic price action, I have found that the stronger and quicker the reversal, the greater potential for a nice move. This is incredibly important because sharp reversals from a PRZ provide clear direction for the future price action. However, price action that is unable to reverse the predominant trend after testing a PRZ frequently is one of the primary signs of a potentially failed or invalid pattern setup.

"You Can Only Profit..."

My good friend Bill Sourbey has repeated the following phrase to me in our discussions of the market through the years:

"You can only profit from that which you can anticipate."

He continually has repeated this principle to me. It has immense relevance to the execution philosophy of harmonic patterns. First, the anticipation of the completion of a pattern establishes the action to be taken. The PRZ defines the limits of the trade, including the execution point, the stop loss limit, and profit target. If a price structure possesses the proper Fibonacci ratio alignment, the anticipation of its completion of the PRZ to validate the pattern creates an *Action-Task Trading Process Model*.

The *Action* involves the preparation and understanding of all of the most pertinent and effective rules for each pattern to successfully trade the opportunity. The *Task* involves executing positions based upon the price action at the completion of the pattern, according to the system of Harmonic Trading rules that defines every possibility, in advance. Does the structure possess the required elements to be a valid pattern? If not, find a setup that does. If so, where does it complete? What happens immediately as the entire completion area is tested? Does the predominant trend continue or does the price action react to the numbers defining the zone?

These are all anticipatory events that have known possible outcomes. Hence, trading tactics within the execution process define a plan that outlines actions for all possible considerations during the trading process.

The **Action** of preparing and determining which positions to execute follows a set of identification rules that quantifies patterns, assesses price action, and defines the parameters of each trade, including the entry, the stop loss and the profit objective. Such preparation is critical to prevent execution mistakes and to determine the optimal entry within the PRZ. Furthermore, thorough preparation is essential when faced with volatile real-time situations, in particular.

Although anything can happen in the financial markets, a thorough understanding of a potential trade's critical technical levels will reduce confusion. For example, extreme price action that clearly violates a PRZ will frequently provide signs of the impending violation. A complete knowledge of the set up and the critical harmonic price levels will reduce losses as pattern failures are spotted well in advance. These situations develop with experience but the task of preparation is an essential part of the trading process for every setup.

The **Task** of execution represents the actualization of the preparation to determine the validity of the opportunity, as defined by the rules of the Harmonic Trading approach. Although the decision of whether or not to execute a trade may seem simple, there are many considerations that may affect the exact entry level or negate the setup altogether. Therefore, the task of execution presents many challenges.

The completion of a pattern creates a unique "technical window," as the nature of price action following the entire test of a Potential Reversal Zone can indicate a great deal about the future price direction of the predominant trend. The action of defining a setup in advance helps to outline the numeric limits of the trade and the technical window, as well. The price action should experience some type of reaction in the PRZ as an early sign of a potential reversal. After a pattern completes, an execution should attempt to capitalize on these small but significantly indicative signals. The ability to interpret a pattern's validity within this technical window will improve with experience, as the same set of circumstances continually manifest traits of a valid reversal well before the big move begins. Although the assessment of price action within this technical window is one of the most challenging aspects of the trading process, the completion of patterns will typically exhibit distinct evidence of whether or not they will fail. Therefore, it is essential to assess harmonic setups within this technical window to determine the task of execution.

It is important to emphasize that the rules within the Harmonic Trading plan are designed to anticipate all possible technical events that have known outcomes. Hence, such trading tactics within the execution process define a plan that addresses all possible actions for each consideration throughout the trading process. However, there is a price to pay in this anticipation. It's called the price of the next tick.

The Price of Technical Information

The price of technical information essentially comes down to the next tick. Depending upon the position, the next tick can make the difference between entering or exiting. If an entry is being prepared, each tick that transpires brings the potential opportunity that much closer (or farther) from the actual realization of the execution. As price action approaches a PRZ, the validity of the pattern must be assessed relative to the current trading behavior. Since the validity of a harmonic pattern depends upon the price action in the PRZ, each price bar that follows the initial test of the PRZ can provide more information regarding the future potential of the existing opportunity. However, a delayed execution in waiting for confirmation of the next tick can often result in missed opportunities.

Every position faces these assessments throughout the entire trading process. It is a type of opportunity cost for that position. If the next tick goes in my favor, I have risked losing one tick during the time of the next decision.

The price of the next tick is best related to reversal situations where a profit target has been attained. For example, let's say you have a profit in a long position but you are considering selling because your targets have been achieved. Due to the profitable positions, greed or fear may stall exit strategies to see "how high will it go?." So, each tick is related in that the next set of data will confirm or deny the current position.

Although it is common to give back some of the reversal to allow breathing room for the price action to assert itself and to determine the extent of the move, the price of technical information must be assessed in comparison with the parameters of the trade. Although this concept will be covered thoroughly in Chapter 11, it is important to understand the decision-making process involved with deciphering price action, especially at the completion of harmonic patterns.

Execution in the Potential Reversal Zone (PRZ)

The essence of Harmonic Trading is executing in the PRZ. As it relates to pattern completions, it is within this "harmonic window" that a great deal of information can be obtained. Remember, harmonic patterns define specific zones that can act as a signpost of potential future price action. If a PRZ of a distinct pattern possesses several numbers in a distinct area, the price range should be considered very harmonic. If the price action reverses from this area, the PRZ could be considered as an important turning point. If the price action does not reverse, it would indicate that the predominant trend is quite strong. The ability to interpret and to decipher the price action within these "harmonic windows" is the determining factor in turning patterns into profits!

Reversal Possibilities

Effective execution requires the discipline to examine a precise PRZ and understand in advance all reversal possibilities.

After executing a position at the completion of a pattern, the price action can do one of three things:

1. **Exceed the PRZ into the Stop Loss Zone.**
2. **Reverse slightly off the PRZ and consolidate.**
3. **Reverse off the PRZ and provide a nice cushion within a relatively short period of time.**

Let's consider the possibilities:

1. The price action moves into the Stop Loss Zone and requires that the loss be taken—next trade. Although this may not be the desired goal, stop losses are a part of the business of trading. Therefore, it is important to remember that all setups are not going to work out. But, if this approach is implemented consistently over the course of many trades, these setups will define a majority of favorable trades.

2. Harmonic setups typically provide some type of initial reaction at a minimum after testing a distinct PRZ. However, all setups are not the same. In this case, when the price action briefly reverses and continues in the predominant trend, it is critical to secure the quick profit before the trade becomes a loss.

3. Price action that reverses for a brief period after testing a PRZ frequently provides a "profit cushion" that provides enough time for the extent of the reversal to be determined. After a small profit is achieved, the trade management techniques are employed to maximize profits and effectively handle the position.

Although this may seem oversimplified, the execution of a trade can result in a profit, loss, or scratch (break even). After a valid harmonic pattern has been identified, the final judgment of whether to pull the trigger can come down to a few price bars. Utilizing the PRZ as the ideal pivot area, the extent of the pattern's validity depends upon specific reversal action within this defined range.

One critical factor in gauging price action in the PRZ can depend upon which numbers are the most important. A convergence of a pattern's projections can be peculiar because in a reversal zone that contains several harmonic calculations, it is difficult to know which point will end the trend. Although these rules are generalized, I believe that they serve as important guidelines to accurately ascertain a priority order of importance to the multitude the harmonic numbers that may comprise a pattern's PRZ.

Potential Reversal Zone (PRZ) Tips

- **Look for an area of convergence.** History has proven that a convergence of Fibonacci ratio projections, especially specific harmonic price patterns, can identify critical technical areas of support and resistance. When a distinct pattern possesses a congregation of ratio projections in a defined price range, it is possible to determine the potential future direction of the trend.

- **Look for where the greatest group of calculations converges.** The key to utilizing these harmonic measures when analyzing a price chart is to determine the area where the greatest group of patterns complete and important ratio calculations converge.

- **The bigger the number the more significant the harmonic area.** The Fibonacci number that is calculated from the largest price leg is usually the most significant at a pattern's completion point. This principle applies to both time and price. For example, a pattern that develops on a weekly chart will be more significant than a setup on a daily basis. Also, if there is a smaller pattern within a larger pattern, the larger pattern usually will be more significant.

- **The amount of numbers within the PRZ.** The number of ratio projections and pattern completions within a specific area will dictate the significance of a particular price level.
- **The proximity of numbers within the PRZ.** If a PRZ possesses several numbers, the ideal area for a pattern's completion and ultimate reversal will likely occur where the majority of the zone's numbers complete.

The proper identification and interpretation of the price action in the PRZ at the completion of a pattern is the defining element for success. The preparation and discipline required to "execute in the zone" is no small task. The determination of a pattern's completion requires patience and practice. The ability to capitalize on the reactive first test of the Potential Reversal Zone is critical in turning patterns into profits. As a pattern completes, the price action can react sharply, requiring a quick assessment and decision of the execution. The key is to be prepared as the price action enters the zone on the initial test.

Entering the PRZ: The Initial Test

A well-defined PRZ usually provides some type of initial reaction on the first test of most harmonic patterns. At a minimum, it has been my experience that distinct PRZs frequently can provide some nominal yet tradable reaction, regardless of the eventual validity of the pattern. Although the extent of the reversal can vary, it is important for the initial reaction to clearly reverse from the entire range of harmonic numbers to validate the pattern.

A common sign of a failed setup is price action that merely consolidates in the PRZ before resuming in the direction of the predominant trend. Although the determination of valid patterns requires some experience to consistently differentiate the winners from the losers, the initial test of the PRZ will always be one of the most critical aspects of the decision-making process. The price bar(s) that form on the initial test will serve as the projected terminal point for measuring the anticipated reversal. These concepts will be covered in actual chart examples later in this material. However, the significance of the price action on the initial test of the PRZ must be emphasized as a vital element of the Harmonic Trading process.

The initial test can occur quickly, and it is not uncommon to miss great pattern completions on the first test due to the volatility of the price action. The best advice I can offer is to be prepared and track a group of potential patterns as trading candidates. Preparation is essential to capitalize on the initial test of distinct pattern completions, as these setups typically offer a reactive yet profitable move.

Many reversal situations experience sharp price action that occurs within a small window of opportunity. For example, it is common for significant long-term patterns to reverse from a PRZ within a day or two after initially testing the zone. This can be frustrating, as a slight distraction could cause the entire trade to be missed. I have encountered many instances where I've missed an anticipated completion of a major intra-day pattern in the index futures like the S&P 500 because I left my screens for 5 minutes to get a cup of coffee. It happens, but the market waits for no one.

Remember, the "harmonic window of opportunity," as defined by the PRZ, is a very precise area that represents the culmination a several significant price movements. The initial test of a PRZ represents the completion of these structures and the anticipated change of the predominant trend. This is significant because, once completed, the potential change in price action can be dramatic. Therefore, it is essential to be prepared in advance to capitalize on these situations. However, even the most prepared trader can still be affected by a common problem of trade execution—hesitation.

The Persimmon Effect

J. M. Hurst, in his profound book *The Profit Magic of Stock Transaction Timing*, eloquently discussed the problem of hesitation or what he called the *Persimmon Effect*:

> *"The ideal time to buy a stock is exactly when it looks the least interesting! Similarly: The ideal time to sell a stock short is when it looks as though it will never stop going up!*
>
> *You will put a stock in your stable and patiently track it for a buy signal. The price continues to drop and the amount of daily or weekly variation dries up along with the volume.*
>
> *Your cyclic (harmonic) analysis tells you to expect this, but it certainly looks as though all investor interest has completely vanished.*
>
> *At such a time it is very difficult indeed to convince yourself that you should actually take action when that buy signal comes along."*
>
> (J. M. Hurst, *The Profit Magic of Stock Transaction Timing* [Greenville, SC: Traders Press, 1970], 163.)

When it comes to trading harmonic patterns, this frequently can happen, especially in the early learning stages. Such hesitation is problematic, although thorough preparation helps to define trading decisions in advance.

Within the Harmonic Trading approach, the problem arises at the completion of patterns, where the "harmonic signal" generated—that is, the test of the PRZ—does not stimulate the appropriate trading action.

Jim Kane of KaneTrading.com and I have discussed the Persimmon Effect extensively in many discussions regarding trade execution. On one particular day, we were looking at a few intra-day patterns in the index futures in the HarmonicTrader.com Chat Room. We were trying to determine if we would get an opportunity to see these patterns complete.

I responded by saying:

> *"WE will always get OUR chance as long as WE give it to OURSELVES."*

Within the Harmonic Trading approach, the opportunity to execute patterns, especially in the PRZ, requires patience and a firm belief in these methods. Although such confidence requires time to maintain the proper perspective, it is essential to realize that we must define our own trading opportunities.

The market will provide the necessary signals that can identify potential trading situations. It's the trader's responsibility to learn what these signals mean and to utilize this technical information to define profitable opportunities. Although other considerations can affect an execution, the degree of success is dependent upon consistently applying the Harmonic Trading techniques to identify opportunities and to turn patterns into profits. The measurement strategies and pattern rules quantify potential opportunities quite effectively. The Harmonic Trading identification techniques consistently pinpoint the optimal price level for a trade execution. However, the physical task of pulling the trigger can present its own set of problems. Despite these inherent challenges throughout the decision-making process, the ultimate step of executing the trade still requires a correct and timely assessment of the price action. Therefore, issues related with trade executions such as hesitation—a.k.a. the Persimmon Effect—should be overcome through the realization as traders that our opportunities and ultimate success is 100% self-dependent.

The hesitation issue also fits well within the **Action/Task Trading Process Model**. As I mentioned previously, the **Action** is defined through the identification and preparation required to define a Harmonic Trading opportunity. The **Task** involves executing positions based upon the general trade management rules that define every possibility, in advance. In essence, hesitation is just the failure to execute the Task.

Although the Persimmon Effect can prevent a trade execution, the solution to the problem can be overcome through a process of learning and emotional conditioning. First, it is important to realize that not all trades are to be taken, even if the opportunity is a distinct harmonic pattern. In fact, in the early application of the Harmonic Trading techniques, it is essential to allow a period of study and preparation to acquire the proper mental perspective. It is important to be well versed in all aspects of the Harmonic Trading approach, knowing all of the identification techniques, the trade execution considerations, and trade management strategies before attempting to integrate these strategies in real-time situations. After a period of study, the basic Harmonic Trading techniques will be obvious. However, the application of this approach requires considerable dedication to develop the analytical skills required to consistently profit from these opportunities.

In my experience, thorough preparation helps to "slow down" the price action in the PRZ. When all trade parameters are defined in advance, the decision process is clear. The "anticipated" trade should act in a specific manner if it is going to be a valid opportunity. Otherwise, the price action is indicating that the pattern is potentially flawed.

This concept of the PRZ as a window of opportunity is incredibly significant. The specific range is the critical "make-or-break" level that determines the validity of a potential pattern. Although there are a variety of confirmation signals to be considered, the basic parameters of the trade as defined by the price points of the pattern elucidate the execution by clearly defining all numeric limits and outlining the make-or-break range for a reversal.

Trade Journal

A trade journal is an effective means of preparation to track potential setups. A trade journal should include the type of pattern, the completion point of the AB=CD, and the Fibonacci retracements within the reversal zone. Also, a written journal is helpful in recording your personal thoughts regarding the relative price action within a reversal zone.

It is important, especially in the early stages of learning these techniques, to keep track of your thoughts. The questions that arise and the ideas generated during the trade execution process are your personal signals that help gauge the price action. It is important to record these feelings and expectations relative to the current price action as a template for comparing what was expected versus what happened. The key to trade execution of harmonic setups still requires the accurate analysis of the price action within the reversal zone. Achieving this "feel for the numbers" requires an understanding of your own personal signals. A trade journal will record your mental processes and trading behavior. It is only through such study that you will improve your executions and become a more successful trader.

I have included a sample of my own journal that shows how I approach trade setups. I line the various setups in "my sights" and wait for them to materialize. If they don't work out the way that I have projected, I move on to the next trade. If I do see a setup that comes together, I gauge the price action. After the opportunity is over, I summarize the events and my response to the opportunity. If I accept a trade, I will record my thoughts and feelings throughout the entire experience until I am out.

October 8th

- **SP500 Mini-Contract (ES_Z9)** = AB=CD @ 1032.75; Down 5 in the pre-market; major 0.618 retracement at 1028.25.
- **Microsoft (MSFT)** = Retesting Bullish Gartley. Look for 0.618 retracement off pattern at $26.
- **Semiconductor Index ($SOX)** = Retesting major Bearish AB=CD. Look to buy calls on retest under 330 area for eventual 0.886 test. Looks like an eventual blowout of this harmonic resistance.
- **NASDAQ 100 Tracking Stock (QQQ):** Setting up Bullish Crab on 60-minute chart in the $33 area in prior daily resistance area. Looks like prior harmonic resistance is offering support.

As you can see by my journal entries, I have identified several trade setups listed as potential opportunities. It is not uncommon for me to follow a potential trade for quite some time, especially when I am tracking price action after a nice harmonic setup.

Trade journals are an effective means to learn a great deal about price action and harmonic set-ups. Most important, a trade journal can teach many lessons about personal insights and perceptions regarding these opportunities. It is even more essential in the beginning stages of your study because each person's trade executions are unique. Although two people may utilize these harmonic methods and calculate the same reversal zone, their execution prices will not be exactly the same. One person might take the trade, while the other avoids it. The difference in the perception of the price action at the pattern's completion point might cause one person to wait for a clear reversal from the zone while another enters the trade in the PRZ without hesitation.

Over time, the trading journal will help you gauge your own personal signals to interpret the market action. You will develop a feel for what "should be happening." For example, let's say that you have identified a valid harmonic set-up with several numbers within a very tight zone. Specifically, you have identified a great Bullish Bat pattern. You are looking to buy but the price action suggests a potentially failed setup because of an extreme price range, tail close, or gap. You might record in the journal that the pattern looks great but the price action at the reversal point is too strong or has a warning signal, so you avoid the trade. Also, you might record that an ideal reversal "should" bounce off this zone quickly and show strong signs, such as a positive close above the harmonic area. In this example, since the stock is not reversing the way it "should," you have not accepted the trade.

During this time, it is important to record the reasons why or why not you accepted the trade, and the emotions that were associated with your actions. Also, after the opportunity has abated, it is important to record how the trade turned out and how you responded to the experience. Did you find yourself biting your nails throughout? Were you feeling confident with your position or did you doubt your analysis? Recording these events helps to instill confidence in your ability to decipher price action and develops technical intuition as a chart reader.

Although not all harmonic setups are ideal, developing certain standards of price action helps create a framework to gauge the reversal zone. A trading journal that records these experiences is the key to developing your intuition. Each person's response to price action is unique. So, it is imperative to learn the signals that you generate during the execution process to improve future trades.

Trading Checklist

At this point, the identification techniques utilized to define harmonic patterns should be common knowledge. There is a simple checklist of requirements that all valid setups must possess.

1. **Is there a pattern?**
2. **What is it?**
3. **Is there an AB=CD?**
4. **Where does it complete?**
5. **Are there three or more numbers converging in the PRZ?**
6. **What are they?**
7. **What are the time cycles (symmetry) suggesting?**
8. **Are there any warning signs?**
9. **At what point is the PRZ no longer valid? (Stop Loss)**
10. **How much must I risk? Am I willing to risk it?**

The guidelines in this section are the result of years of harmonic research. The Harmonic Trading Checklist summaries a complex process of measurement considerations into a concise format. Furthermore, this checklist optimizes trade executions by clearly defining all of the numeric limits of the setup, in advance.

Trade Execution Considerations

When it comes down to the actual execution, several considerations can influence trading behavior. In essence, trading harmonic patterns versus just analyzing harmonic patterns are two different endeavors. The trade execution in the PRZ is frequently a short window of opportunity. Within that time period, a multitude of factors can delay or even cause a trade to be missed. Therefore, effective execution requires a more intense and disciplined approach than just identifying harmonic patterns on a chart.

I would like to take a moment to discuss the distinction between actual trading and simple pattern identification. I trade these patterns almost everyday, and I must emphasize the discipline required to actively trade this methodology. In fact, pattern identification is merely the first step in the process. The degree of trading success requires an ability to identify distinct patterns, to execute trades in the PRZ and to manage positions within the rules of the Harmonic Trading approach in all types of market conditions. Actual trading situations can present challenges that can result in missed trades. Although this can be frustrating, it is better to only execute those pattern completions that offer the clearest price zones. These are a few of the lessons that must be learned before gaining a "realistic perspective" on the entire approach.

20/20 Hindsight

For these reasons, Harmonic Trading frequently looks better in the past than it does in the present or the future. It is easy to identify past patterns in price charts and lay claim to what could have been. Unfortunately, the uncertainties involved with real-time executions frequently alter the true outcome. Furthermore, it can be difficult to know exactly which setups will yield valid reversals. It would be great if "conditional" orders could be executed the day after a valid reversal is confirmed and execute trades exactly at the reversal points. Although such hindsight trading would be immensely profitable, it is possible to interpret the price action at certain harmonic price zones to determine the validity of a reversal.

The problem arises when price action does not act as anticipated or reverse ideally. This can lead to missed trades and create uncertainty about future set-ups. Although these realities are a part of the execution process, there are some considerations that can help attain a "20/20" success level:

1. **Prepare in advance.** It is critical to maintain a list of prospective trades that are approaching their PRZ. Setting software alerts and monitoring setups as they get close to their entry point will improve executions.
2. **Trades will be missed.** Although certain situations may possess seemingly perfect patterns, it is important to note that not all trades should be taken. Extreme price action can warn about invalid setups. Sometimes, setups still reverse in the desired direction, despite these indications.
3. **Use 20/20 hindsight.** The keys to correcting mistakes and developing more effective trading strategies can only be discovered through reviewing prior trades.

Harmonic Trading Psychology

There are numerous books on trading psychology that can outline a variety of techniques to improve the mental aspects of trading. I believe it is an important area of the market to study. But, I would like to offer a few ideas to improve your trading psychology:

- **Keep it simple.** Although there is a definite advantage to learning as much as you can about the markets, overanalysis of potential opportunities can create confusion and second-guessing. It is important to incorporate only those techniques that have clearly proven to be effective tools. Yes, certain indicators can be reliable, but it is ridiculous to try to incorporate every technical measure when assessing a trade.
- **Stick to a winning plan.** They key ingredient in preventing this confusion is to create and stick to a winning trading plan. Although I may consider extraneous variables when assessing a potential trade, Harmonic Trading techniques as defined in my trading plan are the fundamental basis for entering a position.

    W. D. Gann discussed the importance of a trading plan in many of his writings:

    > *"Have a well-defined plan before you start trading, then follow that plan, as the architect does in building a house, or the engineer in constructing a bridge or driving a tunnel.*
    >
    > *The man who changes his ideas or his plan, which are based on something practical, for no other reason than that he hopes or fears the market will do something different, will never make a success."*

    (*Truth of the Stock Tape* [Pomeroy, WA: Lambert-Gann Publishing, 1923]).

- **Full-time trading is not a full-time job.** One of the most common reasons for lacking a clear mental perspective is the simple fact that many traders trade too much. Could you stop trading for more than a week? A month? A year even? Or do you have to trade? If you have to trade, you might as well go to Las Vegas because you have just entered the world of a gambling addict. It is important to take a break after a certain period of time and pace your trading efforts.

- **Study the masters.** In my desire to learn the most pertinent information on the market, I discovered many books that were more than 50 years old that contained incredible market insights that remain valid to this day. Today's "pop trading" books have been penned by high-profile market celebrities. Unfortunately, many of these people are not active traders. In fact, at the first online trade show that I attended I met with several notable authors. It was amazing that many of these people were not active traders, and many stated that they have not traded for years. Authors such as W. D. Gann, J. M. Hurst, and R. N. Elliott contain pertinent insights into past markets that are as effective as they were 100 years ago.

- **Review your work.** The only way to overcome your trading errors is to study your trades. Although losses are a part of the business of trading, it essential to review those trades and the mistakes that caused the faulty judgment to prevent repeating the same mistakes. If you must pay tuition at the University of Wall Street to learn how to trade successfully, you have to do your homework and review your mistakes. Otherwise, you will be doomed to repeat them.

- **Don't care.** The proper psychology required in the execution of any trade should entail an almost careless attitude. After defining all trade parameters (entry, exit, stop loss) in advance, the pure execution of the trade should be nearly emotionless. Such an attitude can be difficult because the money risked in each trade can stimulate fear or greed. However, the key is to focus on the price action before, during and after a pattern has completed. Any other thoughts, emotions or considerations outside the realm of the price action at the completion of the defined pattern are meaningless. Furthermore, it is really not about money. This is a game of strategy and tactic. The level of success depends upon the proper application of an effective approach such as the Harmonic Trading methods to turn patterns into profits

Trading Questionnaire

This list of questions is an excellent means to review your overall trading goals. A personal assessment review is effective in that it can outline your personal beliefs and basic expectations of trading in general. I recommend writing answers to these questions and incorporating these guidelines into your overall trading plan:

1. **Why do you want to trade?**
2. **When was the first time you realized you wanted to trade? Why?**
3. **What was your first trade?**
4. **What was your last trade?**
5. **What was your best trade ever?**
6. **What was your worst?**
7. **What is your preferred time frame for trading? (Day/Position/Investor)**
8. **What is your greatest benefit of trading outside of the money?**
9. **What is your greatest fear associated with trading?**
10. **How do you know when to buy/short a stock?**
11. **How do you know when to cover that position?**

12. **What is your greatest strength in your trading?**
13. **What is your greatest weakness?**
14. **What areas of trading do you think you need to learn more about?**
15. **Do you review your past trades?**
16. **What do you expect to get out of trading? (List three accomplishments.)**
17. **What will your trading be like within each of the following time periods?**
    - **Six months**
    - **One year**
    - **Five years**

Effective trade execution requires discipline and preparation. Although a variety of mental aspects are involved in the decision-making process, the rules that define harmonic setups must serve as the foundation for all trading behavior. Executing in the PRZ and identifying patterns with three harmonic numbers in a specific area are examples of the types of basic rules that must be consistently followed if success is to be achieved. These questions should be reviewed from time to time, as a follow-up to your trading progress.

Chapter 10

Price Action in the Potential Reversal Zone (PRZ)

Ideal Reversals

An ideal reversal usually possesses several characteristics that clearly separate it from other types of price reactions. An ideal reversal usually tests all of the numbers in a Potential Reversal Zone on the initial test. The predominant trend usually reverses from this initial test of the entire PRZ and continues in the reversal direction shortly thereafter. In an ideal reversal, the price bar that tests all of the numbers in the PRZ is called the *Terminal Price Bar* (T-bar).

Ideal Bullish Reversal

In an ideal bullish reversal, the price action should reverse after the entire range is tested (see Figure 10.1). Although price action may seem strong as it declines into the Potential Reversal Zone, the critical determining point is the reaction of the predominant trend at the completion of the pattern. The Terminal Price Bar should stabilize after completing the test.

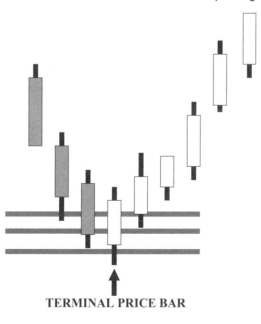

TERMINAL PRICE BAR

Figure 10.1

Dow Jones Industrial Average
(^DJI): Weekly

The Dow Jones Industrial Average formed this Bullish Bat after retracing the initial rally of the 2003 low following an extended three-year decline from the 2000 peak (see Figure 10.2).

Figure 10.2

The index tested the entire PRZ on the week it completed the pattern. Although the weekly candlestick represented the Terminal Price Bar for the pattern, the following chart of the price action in the PRZ in Figure 10.3 shows an ideal reversal on the daily time frame.

Figure 10.3

Clearly, the index established the T-bar on the day it tested the entire PRZ. It is important to note that the sell-off was quite severe as the price action approached the harmonic support. Despite the extreme decline, the Dow Jones Industrials stabilized and reversed nicely after the Terminal Price Bar was established.

Ideal Bearish Reversal

In an ideal bearish reversal, the price action should reverse after the entire range is tested (see Figure 10.4). Although price action may seem strong as it rallies toward the Potential Reversal Zone, the critical determining point is the reaction of the predominant trend at the completion of the pattern.

TERMINAL PRICE BAR

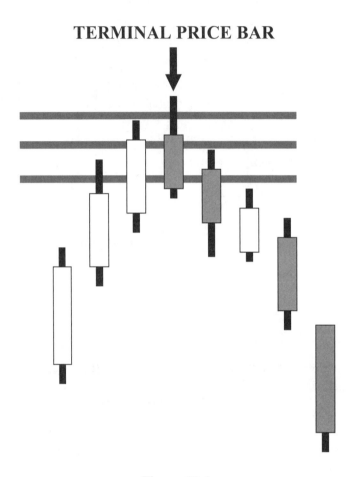

Figure 10.4

The most ideal bearish situations continue immediately to the downside after the entire PRZ is tested and the T-bar is established. The Terminal Price Bar should close below the range of harmonic numbers in the best cases.

Pepsi (PEP): 15-Minute

Pepsi completed this Bearish Butterfly on the following 15-minute chart (see Figure 10.5). The stock rallied sharply into the PRZ but stalled after testing all of the numbers.

Figure 10.5

The reversal in this case exemplified an ideal situation, especially with the Terminal Price Bar being clearly established after testing the entire range of harmonic numbers. The chart of the price action in the Potential Reversal Zone in Figure 10.6 marks the T-bar with the arrow. The dotted line marks the top of the Terminal Price Bar, defining the price level that would negate the harmonic resistance established by the pattern. Essentially, a violation above this level would question the validity of the trade, and it could even trigger a reversal of the pattern to get long on a breakout above this area. I will cover these strategies later in this material. For now, it is important to focus on the elements that define a Terminal Price Bar and the type of reversal that should occur after it has been established.

Figure 10.6

Warning Signs in the Potential Reversal Zone (PRZ)

It is common for price action to exhibit extreme signs warning in invalid harmonic patterns. In many situations, as the price action enters into a PRZ, price gaps and extreme extension moves can be the trigger of failed setups. Although valid patterns may possess price action that is extreme, warning signs like these must be considered when assessing the validity of a PRZ. I refer to these situations as "blowouts," since warning signs can frequently trigger blatant and convincing price behavior that invalidates the projected completion of a harmonic pattern.

Price Gaps Through the Potential Reversal Zone (PRZ)

Price gaps at the completion of harmonic patterns are a common development that must be handled carefully. Patterns like the Crab frequently possess sharp price action in their PRZ. Despite these situations, the determining factor is the extent of the price gap as the action tests the PRZ.

Price Gap Through a Bullish Potential Reversal Zone (PRZ)

As price action approaches the harmonic support defined by the PRZ, it typically will "bypass" the entire range of numbers on a price gap that invalidates the pattern. A price gap THROUGH the PRZ, as Figure 10.7 demonstrates, is quite different from a price gap INTO the PRZ. The obvious price gap-warning signal occurs when the price action trades completely past the PRZ, failing to test any other numbers.

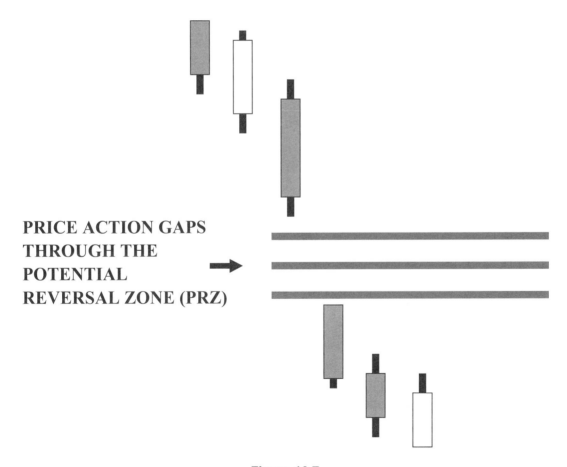

PRICE ACTION GAPS THROUGH THE POTENTIAL REVERSAL ZONE (PRZ)

Figure 10.7

Wal-Mart
(WMT): Daily

The daily chart of Wal-Mart in Figure 10.8 demonstrates extreme price action that trades completely through the harmonic support established by the completion of the Bullish Gartley.

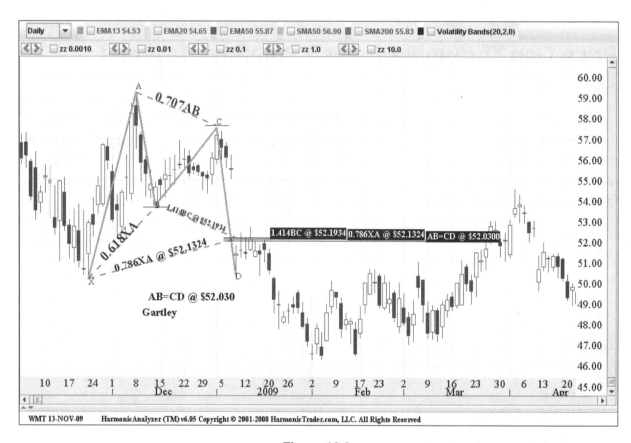

Figure 10.8

The blowout in this case exemplified the ideal price gap-warning signal. The stock opened below the PRZ, gapping down past the critical range of numbers at the completion of the pattern. The 52.20 level was an extremely critical harmonic support level, as the three numbers converged in a narrow PRZ. Since the stock opened below these numbers and rolled over quickly a few days later, the validity of the pattern was negated. Again, it is important to focus on the action on the initial test of the harmonic numbers. Although the stock bounced a few days following the violation, the price gap on the open through the entire PRZ exemplified this warning signal (see Figure 10.9).

Figure 10.9

Another important element of a blowout is the action that follows the violation. Clearly, a price bar that blows out a PRZ, trading completely past the numbers, invalidates the projected completion point. However, it is common for price gaps to materialize IN a PRZ but still yield a valid reversal. In these cases, it is best to wait for the following price bar to provide further evidence of the extent of the action. The action will frequently continue in the predominant trend immediately after the test of the PRZ if the pattern is invalid. These issues will be covered further in the Trade Management section later in this material. For now, the clear violation of a price gap THROUGH the entire PRZ will negate a completion point of the pattern.

Blowout of Bearish Potential Reversal Zone (PRZ)

Bearish blowouts that gap through harmonic resistance zones commonly offer obvious warning signals, if the projected completion of the pattern is invalid (see Figure 10.10). In many instances, price gaps that blowout bearish PRZs can act as tremendous continuation signals to follow the predominant trend.

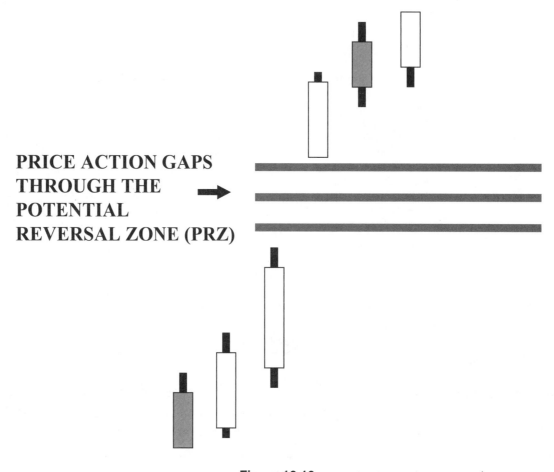

PRICE ACTION GAPS THROUGH THE POTENTIAL REVERSAL ZONE (PRZ) →

Figure 10.10

As was the case with the bullish illustration, the blowout of a bearish PRZ should trade through the entire group of harmonic numbers and continue in the predominant trend. These situations should be practically obvious, as the price action should rally sharply above the projected resistance area.

Microsoft (MSFT): 60-Minute

Microsoft blew out this Bearish Crab on the 60-minute chart, as the stock gapped through the PRZ on the open and immediately continued higher (see Figure 10.11).

Figure 10.11

The blowout in this case exemplified the ideal price gap-warning signal that typically invalidates setups. After the stock opened above these numbers, the validity of the pattern was negated. Again, it is important to focus on the action on the initial test of the harmonic numbers. Although the stock briefly retested the top range of the zone, the strong continuation following the violation confirmed the warning signal provided by the price gap. The chart of the price action in the PRZ in Figure 10.12 shows the clear violation of the price gap and the immediate bullish continuation.

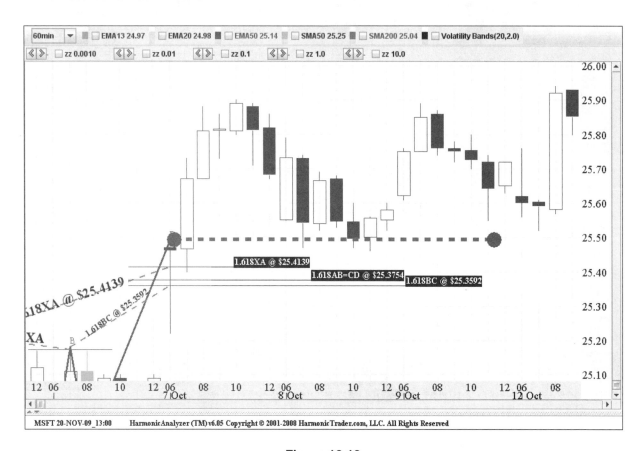

Figure 10.12

It is uncanny how frequently these situations occur, signaling an invalid pattern completion. These warning signs should appear nearly obvious, as the price action should convincingly take out the PRZ.

Extreme Price Expansion Through a Potential Reversal Zone (PRZ)

Frequently, an invalid setup will be indicated by extreme price expansion moves that quickly trade through the PRZ and continue in the predominant trend. Although it might be difficult to validate such an extreme expansion until after the fact, the critical factor is the general momentum that the initial test possesses as it trades into the PRZ. Such extreme price expansion should be followed by a clear continuation of that predominant trend.

Extreme Price Expansion—Bullish Potential Reversal Zone (PRZ)

In an extreme price expansion through a bullish PRZ, the trading should clearly and decisively break down through the support zone on the initial test and continue lower in the predominant trend after the violation (see Figure 10.13).

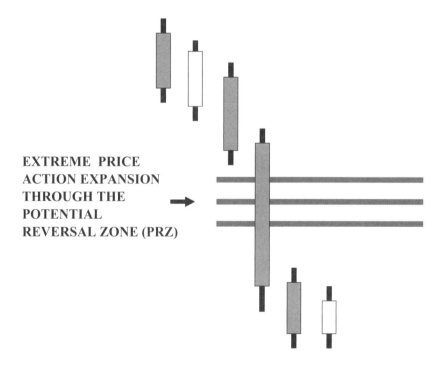

EXTREME PRICE ACTION EXPANSION THROUGH THE POTENTIAL REVERSAL ZONE (PRZ)

Figure 10.13

The breakdown should occur quickly and be practically obvious during the test of the PRZ. As is the case for most PRZ tests, the determining factor is the price action after the entire range of numbers has been tested. If the price action continues sharply lower after the dramatic violation, the completion point of the pattern should be considered invalid.

Coca-Cola (KO): Weekly

The weekly chart in Figure 10.14 shows a Bullish Gartley that possessed a sharp decline as it tested the entire Potential Reversal Zone.

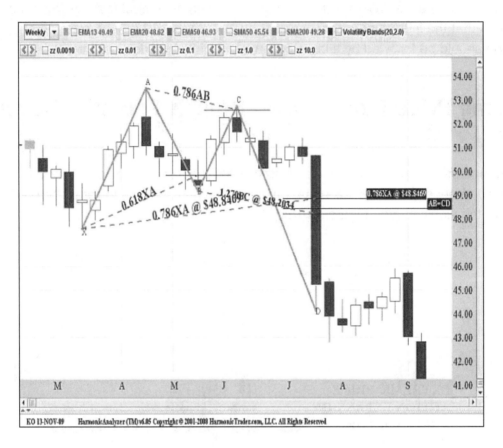

Figure 10.14

Figure 10.15 of the price action in the PRZ exemplifies the extreme price expansion that clearly signaled an invalid setup. As the stock traded into the PRZ, it quickly violated the critical numbers at the completion of the pattern. After the initial test violated the entire range of the harmonic numbers, Coke continued decisively lower.

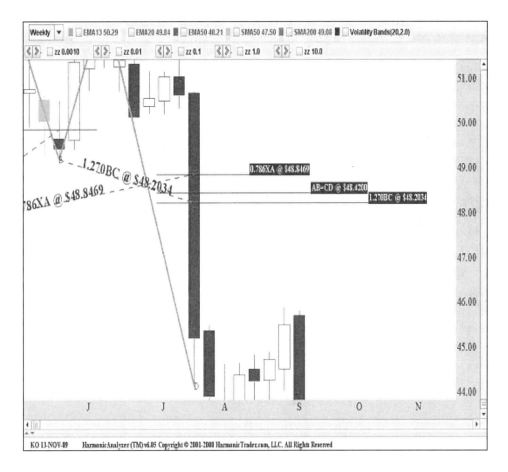

Figure 10.15

The setup was clearly violated, as the severity of the violation was overwhelming. The validity of the harmonic support defined by the PRZ revealed itself quickly after the pattern completed.

Price Action Expansion—Bearish Potential Reversal Zone (PRZ)

Extreme price expansions that break out above bearish PRZs frequently signal a continuation of the predominant trend (see Figure 10.16). The price action should trade decisively through the resistance area and continue to rally following the violation.

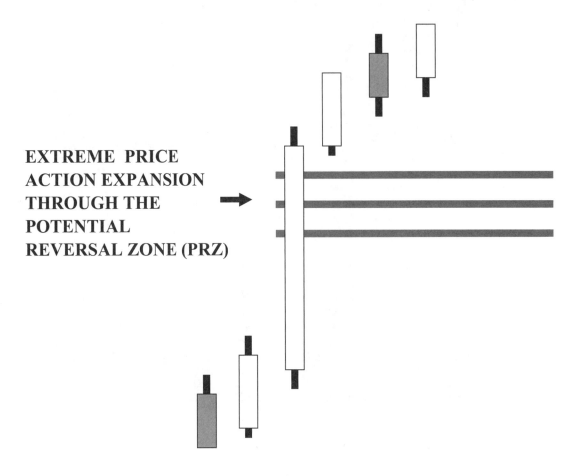

EXTREME PRICE ACTION EXPANSION THROUGH THE POTENTIAL REVERSAL ZONE (PRZ)

Figure 10.16

Again, it might be difficult to validate such an extreme expansion until after the fact. The deciding factor is the price action immediately after the entire PRZ has been tested. If the price action rallies with strong momentum, it is likely that the warning sign is indicating an invalid pattern setup. Any trading that continues higher will confirm this signal.

Dow Jones Industrial Average ($INDU): 15-Minute

Figure 10.17 is an ideal example of the extreme price expansion warning of an invalid setup. The Dow Jones Industrials formed this Bearish Gartley on the following 15-minute chart that rallied through the entire PRZ as it tested the convergence of harmonic numbers just above 9900.

Figure 10.17

___

_____

Figure 10.18 of the price action in the PRZ shows an ideal blowout of the extreme expansion bar. It is important to note that the index closed above the top range of the PRZ and continued higher immediately following the confirmation of the blowout of the bearish pattern.

Figure 10.18

Price Action in the Potential Reversal Zone (PRZ) Conclusion

One of the key principles of Harmonic Trading is analyzing the price action within precise zones as defined by a convergence of Fibonacci calculations of specific 5-point structures. The type of price bars that form at the completion of a pattern can provided extensive information regarding the potential state of the future trading action. In this example, the price action in the Dow Jones Industrials overwhelmingly indicated a pattern failure. Although such interpretation requires some experience, it is important to respect clear violation signals to differentiate valid reversals from failures.

Chapter 11

The Harmonic Trade Management System

I want to review the trade that forced me to create this system because it was a real heartbreaker. It probably was one of the greatest moves that I've ever missed. The stock: Redhat—RHAT! I remember thinking before I entered this trade that the symbol alone was a sign of a bad trade—a dirty RHAT! I thought that it might be a loser, despite the overwhelming harmonics.

The trade involved a nice bullish AB=CD at a critical 0.618 retracement that defined the area just under $75 as significant harmonic support (see Figure 11.1). Despite my apprehension for the symbol, I placed my trade. I bought 1200 shares at 74 3/4. Within a day or two, the stock rallied vigorously. The stock moved sideways for several days after the initial bounce.

Figure 11.1

With the lack of follow-through, I immediately covered the position. I was up nearly 15 points at the high and felt compelled to take my profits and run. I was very happy with this trade. I felt that this move would not continue much higher—was I ever wrong! The chart in Figure 11.2 of price action in the Potential Reversal Zone (PRZ) clearly shows the ideal reversal after testing all of the numbers in the harmonic support zone.

Figure 11.2

Despite stalling for nearly two weeks after the initial reversal, RHAT eventually rallied considerably higher, more than doubling in the following month. Yes, say it with me: "An easy hundred thousand left on the table!" You can see why I felt compelled to develop a system that would respond to market signals rather than emotional reactions.

Although I missed out on these profits, I was determined to learn from this experience. If I was not going to directly profit from this trade, I made it a point to learn from yet another tuition payment to the University of NASD! It was the only way I could overcome my anguish over missing a "lottery trade."

I learned several important factors from this trade that helped me distinguish the big moves from the small reactions. I noticed specific traits in the price action that led me to explore and experiment with different ideas that effectively gauged the strength of the reversal. Techniques such as trend lines, Fibonacci targets, and trailing stops are effective tools that can improve trading decisions. Furthermore, these strategies create a systematic approach to maximize trading decisions in any market environment.

The experience with RHAT forced me to develop a trade management system that truly lets the price action provide the signals to handle the position. Essentially, if you do not have rules to determine the information that the market is providing, you are closing positions based mostly on emotional decisions. Think about it—what was the last trade you closed out? Why? Was it because you didn't think the market would go completely your way? Were you burned by a previous trade that compelled you to take the quick profit or cut the loss small? Quite simply in the case of the RHAT trade, I failed to follow through, as I did not have any technical reasons to close the position.

In the same sense that effective pattern recognition rules—the Harmonic Trading techniques—are employed to identify potential opportunities, it is critical to have guidelines that maximize the management of positions and gauge the price action after a setup has been executed. The trade management rules address all possibilities in advance, enables you to respond to any situation, and instills confidence in your execution skills.

The Harmonic Trade Management Terms

Review these terms to understand the concepts of this system.

Potential Reversal Zone (PRZ)

The Potential Reversal Zone (PRZ) is a specific area where harmonic patterns complete and Fibonacci projections converge. Identification of a valid PRZ is dependent upon finding the clearest pattern structures that possess several Fibonacci calculations converging at a well-defined price level. Also, it is important to remember that a PRZ represents a significant "potential" reversal area and a violation of that area indicates that the primary trend is strong. Therefore, the validity of the setup still requires an accurate assessment of the pattern after the entire zone has been tested.

Initial Profit Objective (IPO)

The Initial Profit Objective (IPO) represents the first area to consider taking profits for the position. Typically, an original position can be parceled into multiple pieces, treating each portion differently depending upon the reversal. The first part of the position—the IPO—is defined by a predetermined Fibonacci level retracement, as measured by the limits (high and low) of the pattern. Most frequently, it is either a 38.2% or 61.8% retracement from the extreme points of the pattern. Also, the IPO can be a trend line violation after the initial target has been exceeded. After a reversal has completed and a small profit has been attained, it is critical to determine the area where the first profit will be secured. The decision to secure the initial profit at the 38.2% or the 61.8% retracement of the pattern range depends upon the price action. If a reversal exceeds the 38.2% level in strong "blowout" fashion by a price gap, extreme price range, or tail close, the 61.8% level should be targeted as the IPO. At a minimum, it is prudent to secure a partial profit at one of these levels.

The blowout of these levels is dependent upon a continuation of the trend. If price action reverses from the PRZ and hits one of the IPO levels but fails to clearly continue in that direction, it is important to cover a part or all of the position. A lack of continuation in the price action is a sign of temporary exhaustion that must be respected. The IPO establishes the initial exit strategy within the Harmonic Trade Management process.

Portioning the IPO

As I mentioned previously, it is customary to split the position into two or even three portions. Such a strategy can secure a profit automatically (with a limit order), ensuring a winning trade on part of the initial position, while creating a "comfort zone" for the other half of the position. The other advantage to splitting the position into two parts is that the other half can "ride for free" after securing an initial profit. Since anything can happen in the market, the other half keeps the position live until the price action signals obvious evidence that it's time to cover. This is critical because it reduces the amount "left on the table." Also, this strategy shifts your trading behavior to respond to the market rather than your own emotions. Although the example of Redhat is an extraordinary case, it underscores the importance of leaving a portion of the original position in long enough to capitalize on the potential of a more significant reversal. Reversals that move sideways after an initial reaction can frequently appear to not yield a substantial move, only to really get moving after a delayed period of consolidation. In this instance, the initial profit is secured by the first 1/2 of the position while maintaining the other portion to permit more time to see if the reversal will continue in the direction of the initial reaction. Regardless of the outcome, the second position lets the market determine the result of the trade. If the price action resumes the reversal, the second position can capitalize on the additional gains and employ greater price objectives for further profit management. If the reversal fails, the trade can be exited with a small profit. This area is referred to as the Profit Protection Zone (PPZ).

Profit Protection Zone (PPZ)

Although this is a bit more subjective in the management of a trade, the Profit Protection Zone (PPZ) is a predetermined level beyond the execution point after a small profit has been achieved. The PPZ is critical because it enforces one of the most important rules within the Harmonic Trading approach:

"Never let a profit become a loss."

It is important to note that not all setups yield the same reversal. Some setups will react for a short period of time and then continue in the predominant trend. These setups can provide a quick move and a small profit, as long as the make-or-break price level is defined. Sometimes, price action can consolidate in the reversal zone and trigger the position to be covered, only to have the reversal resume its move. Although these are frustrating situations, the PPZ will prevent the common mistakes of staying in a position that eventually fails.

Stop Loss Zone (SLZ)

The Stop Loss Zone (SLZ) is the area beyond the Potential Reversal Zone that defines an invalid setup. When price action exceeds a reversal zone, it indicates that the PRZ is not a valid turning point, requiring that the position be covered and the loss to be taken.

The 0.382 Trailer

The 0.382 trailing stop is a technique that was initially discussed in *The Harmonic Trader* and developed after studying the Redhat trade closely. The trailing stop is typically employed after a profit has been attained in a position. The 38.2% trailer represents the "make-or-break" limit for the continuation of a reversal. This trailing stop is typically utilized after the Initial Profit Objective (IPO) has been attained.

The 0.382 trailer is measured from the reversal point to the reversal extreme—high (bullish setup) or low (bearish setup). The 0.382 is significant because the strongest price action will only retrace to this level before continuing in the trend of the reversal. Although it is common for the reversal trend to frequently retest this retracement, the critical technical consideration is a violation beyond this area. Therefore, the position should be covered on a continuation past the 38.2% level.

Trend Lines

There are two types of trend lines that are utilized in trade management decisions. After the initial reversal from a Potential Reversal Zone, it is common for price action to adhere to a general trend line that can serve as a gauge of the potential continuation of the new move. Trend lines can be effective in catching reversals that provide brief reactions but revert to the predominant trend. Although brief reactions from well-defined patterns occur frequently, these temporary moves can provide quick profitable trades, if they are handled properly.

The other trend line consideration involves the Initial Profit Objective (IPO), usually at the 38.2% or 61.8% pattern retracement. In most setups, the 0.382 IPO typically converges with a trend line from the existing pattern. For example, a bullish pattern will possess a down trend line from the high points (A and C) that can be drawn to define the predominant trend's resistance channel. In combination with the IPO, this area represents the "line in the sand." If a reversal can exceed the initial profit objective, the probability is favorable for a more significant move than just a temporary reaction. Although this rule allows for some discretion, the initial profit area is crucial in differentiating the big moves from the small reactions well in advance.

Angle of Ascent/Descent

The angle of ascent/descent refers to the degree of the trend line of the price action after it has reversed from the completion of the pattern. Although the angle does not need to be precisely measured, it is important to note that most valid reversals will frequently possess steep trend lines with decisive continuation. In comparison, price action that moves sideways at the completion of a pattern is typically an early sign of an impending failure.

Time Considerations

After the initial reversal from a PRZ, a certain amount of time is required to allow the price action to assert itself and begin a new trend. Whether the pattern forms on a 5-minute, 60-minute, daily, or weekly chart, each reversal must be allotted a certain time period relative to the size of the pattern to manifest signals of its validity.

As I discussed in the beginning of the book, each pattern must be regarded as a specific *technical entity* that possesses precise numeric ranges, where all elements, such as execution points, stop loss limits, and profit objectives, are defined relative to the structure. These established price parameters apply to the time considerations, as well.

Although time considerations are not as significant as the factors of price, an understanding of when a setup should complete can optimize trade management decisions and offer relevant technical confirmation of a reversal's potential.

There is a general "window of time" that should be considered after a reversal has completed. The acceptable limits of pattern completions are comprised of two time measurements—the equivalent time completion and alternate time calculations—that are critical in the decision-making process of trade management.

The equivalent time projection is a general estimation of the completion of a symmetrical pattern. Utilizing the X point as the initial starting point, the time duration is measured to the pattern's mid-point (B). This time duration is projected from the B point to determine the approximate D point completion. Ideally, the most symmetrical patterns will complete at the equivalent completion time. For example, if a pattern required ten days to form the X to B point, the B to D point projected time completion should be ten days thereafter. In a similar fashion as a perfect AB=CD pattern, the time symmetry should be equivalent.

The alternate time calculation is calculated with the range of Harmonic Trading ratios, starting with 0.382 and extending to 1.618. In many patterns, the CD leg frequently does not complete before the equivalent projected time date. Although the symmetry may be less than ideal in these situations, a proper alignment of Fibonacci ratios is still the critical requirement to validate any potential pattern setup.

At a minimum, a pattern should not complete until it has reached the 0.382 time projection. For example, if the time distance to the mid-point of a pattern (from X to B) is ten days, the pattern should not complete until the distance from B the projected completion has traded for 3.82 or approximately four days. Although this is a rule that should be applied generally with some room for interpretation, this minimum 38.2% projected time requirement serves as a filter for potentially invalid patterns. Essentially, if a pattern possesses a sharp CD leg that completes in a relatively short period of time as compared to the rest of the price structure, a red flag should go up and the validity of the setup must be considered suspect.

Although there are many other time considerations that should be assessed in the trade management process, I believe this basic understanding of a projected "time window" promotes the proper anticipation of price action and establishes the model of "what should be happening" in a valid reversal. Basically, the projected time window defines the accepted duration of the reversal, creating a "do or die" perspective.

The equivalent time projection helps to define the PPZ. The decision to protect a small profit versus allowing more time for a trade to reverse is dependent upon the equivalent time completion of the pattern. Within this "time window," the price action either reverses within the time allotted or the reversal at hand must become suspect. In these circumstances, small profits must be defended. Although this may be mentally frustrating, small profits are better than sitting on your hands and allowing a loss.

The concept of the PPZ evolved from many personal experiences with patterns that provided an initial reaction, only to continue in the predominant trend. As I have said throughout this material, most distinct patterns will provide some type of reaction at a minimum.

The ability to profit from these situations depends upon an honest assessment of the price action within the PPZ. Although such defensive tactics can result in a covered position that eventually reverses in the anticipated direction, in the long run this strategy is one of the most effective tools within the Harmonic Trade Management System.

It will take some time to grasp the intricacies of these trade management techniques. However, the system defines all possible parameters of the trade relative to the pattern and the price action in the PRZ. It is essential to establish entry points, profit targets, and stop loss limits well in advance to facilitate the decision-making process.

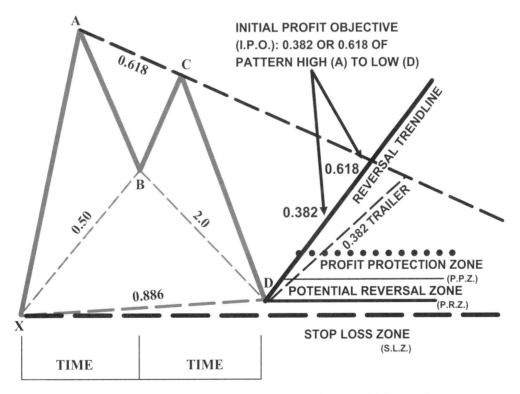

Figure 11.3 *(Copyright HarmonicTrader.com, LLC, 2010)*

General Electric (GE): Daily

The chart in Figure 11.4 was sent with the original trade recommendation to all HarmonicTrader.com members on October 17, 2003 via the Email Advisory section of the website. As the chart illustrates, GE was forming a distinct Bullish Bat on the daily chart.

Figure 11.4

In the email, I wrote:

> *"General Electric (GE) is approximately 1 point from the Potential Reversal Zone (PRZ) of a Bullish Bat with three numbers between 27.50-28. I would look to buy the stock in this PRZ below $28. The stop loss should be placed at 25.50, risking approximately 2 points in the trade. This is a short-term trade with an initial profit objective of 32.80."*

(To review the actual recommendation, please go to http://www.HarmonicTrader.com/members/harmonic/email/gebatbull.htm.)

The defining level was clearly the convergence of the 0.886 XA retracement at 27.50 and the 1.618 BC projection at 27.65 (see Figure 11.5). Although the Alternate 1.27 AB=CD completed at 28.05, the other numbers pointed to the area under $28.

Figure 11.5

Although certain numbers within a PRZ may possess greater significance than others, the entire range of numbers must be considered more than a single price point. After testing the entire PRZ, the optimal execution area for the trade will depend upon the nature of the price action at the pattern's completion point.

The chart in Figure 11.6 of price action in the PRZ shows an ideal reversal after a complete test of this range. On November 18, the trade was executed at the 0.886 retracement at 27.50. GE reversed on this day after slightly exceeding the bottom of the PRZ.

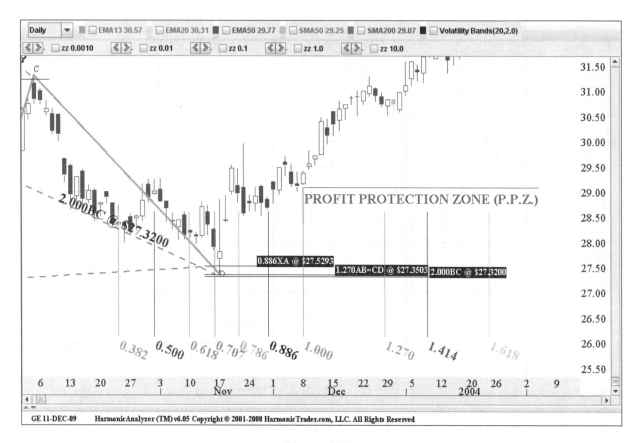

Figure 11.6

The spread of Fibonacci numbers at the bottom of the chart represents the basic mid-point time projection completions for the pattern. Although the CD leg completed after the minimum 0.382 time projection, the equivalent (1.0) calculation was not reached until a few weeks after the reversal was complete (see Figure 11.7).

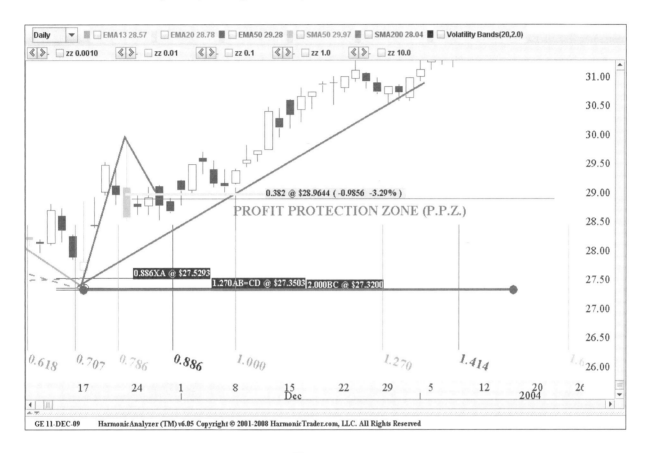

Figure 11.7

Although GE rallied the day following the reversal, as the stock gapped up and continued higher, the more substantial breakout move did not occur until after the equivalent time projection (1.0) was reached.

Figure 11.8 is a classic example of importance of time when assessing the Profit Protection Zone (PPZ). Up until the equivalent time projection completion, any small profit should have been defended. Essentially, GE needed to get going beyond the equivalent time projection completion, if this Bullish Bat was going to yield a significant reversal.

Figure 11.8

After hitting the equivalent time projection completion, the stock started to break out and rally toward the 0.382 Initial Profit Objective (IPO) at 29.50. The downtrend line from the peak of the pattern converged with the IPO, confirming the importance of this resistance.

The first upside target in the $29.50 area was taken out, while maintaining a steady uptrend from the low. The next target at the 0.618 was quickly reached, as GE rallied impressively and with a strong bullish continuation. On November 24th, the stop loss was moved from (27.50) to 28.50, securing 1 point. On December 18th, the stop loss was moved from 28.50 to 30, securing 3 points, establishing a wider PPZ (see Figure 11.8). Beyond this point, the position should be held, as long as the uptrend and the 0.382 trailing stop remain intact. The real work in a valid pattern like this Bullish Bat is monitoring the price action in the PRZ and the corresponding reaction after the reversal has completed.

In this case for GE, the price and time limits were clearly defined in advance. The setup possessed a distinct bullish pattern to buy the stock in the 27.50–28 level. The stock reversed ideally after the entire range of numbers was tested. Beyond the execution, the trade management was quite simple. The Harmonic Trade Management system effectively handled the setup by allowing the reversal to ride while utilizing a well-defined uptrend line and a 0.382 trailing stop as the exit strategy.

Although the 0.382 and 0.618 profit targets were exceeded convincingly, it is still important to monitor the price levels as measured from the pattern's high point to reversal low to establish new price objectives, especially as the reversal moves further. Beyond the 0.618, the price measurements of the 0.786, 0.886, 1.0, 1.27, and so on should be considered as well. The spread of Harmonic Trading ratios is illustrated in Figure 11.8.

NASDAQ 100 December 2003 Mini-Contract (NQ_Z3): 30-Minute

The NASDAQ December 2003 Mini-contract formed the Bullish Crab in Figure 11.9 on a 30-minute chart. I outlined this harmonic support in my pre-market Mini-Room post on HarmonicTrader.com November 19, 2003. I discussed the importance of the 1360 area for the NQ stating. In the email, I stated,

> *"For today's immediate action, the NQ is up 6 1/2. I expect the NQ to try to refill today's upside gap....I would look to buy the NQ after a reversal from this retest in the 1360 area for a move back to 1375."*

(To review the actual recommendation, please go to http://www.HarmonicTrader.com/members/harmonic/home/miniroom111903.htm.)

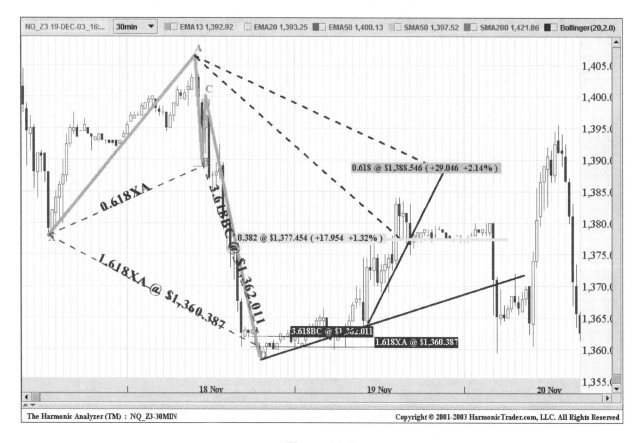

Figure 11.9

The setup possessed a convergence of numbers that defined the 1360 area as critical short-term support. The most significant number at pattern's completion point was the 1.618 XA projection at 1360.40. The 3.618 BC projection at 1362 complemented this harmonic support.

The chart in Figure 11.10 of the price action in the PRZ shows an ideal reversal after a complete test of this harmonic support range. Although the NQ declined sharply into this PRZ, it clearly stabilized and reversed almost exactly from the lower range of the harmonic support.

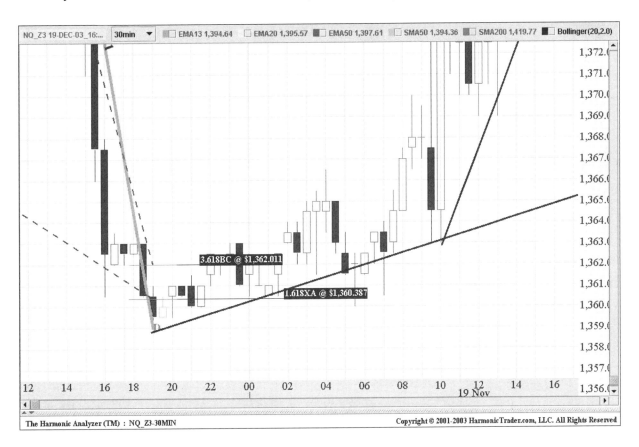

Figure 11.10

The interesting aspect of this reversal was the time consideration at the pattern's completion. The chart in Figure 11.10 shows the spread of Fibonacci time calculations, as measured from the mid-point (B) and projected to the completion of the pattern.

Initially, the CD leg of the Crab pattern completed at the minimum 0.382 time projection. Although this marked the low in the reversal, the price action required more time to stabilize, consolidate, and rally from the PRZ. It was not until the equivalent (1.0) time projection was reached that the reversal started to rally dramatically (see Figure 11.11).

Figure 11.11

The first upside target for the trade was the 1377 area at the 0.382 IPO as measured from the pattern. The NQ exceeded this target, maintaining a steady uptrend throughout the day. Despite the impressive rally through the 0.382 IPO, the NQ stalled, as it failed to test the next target at the 0.618 and violated the intra-day uptrend line (see Figure 11.12).

Figure 11.12

Such a lack of continuation and violation of a distinct trend line are clear signs of a stalling reversal. In this case, especially in a day trade, the long position should be covered.

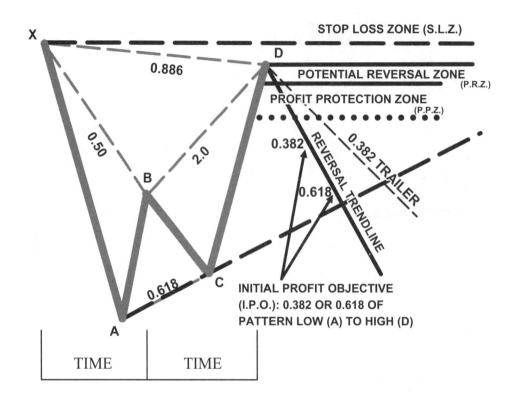

Bearish Harmonic Trade Management Model

Figure 11.13

Standard and Poor's 500 September 2003
Mini-Contract
(ES_U3): 15-Minute

The Standard and Poor's 500 September 2003 Mini-contract formed this Bearish Gartley on the 15-minute chart shown in Figure 11.14. The setup possessed a convergence of three numbers between 1018 and 1019.25 that defined critical short-term resistance.

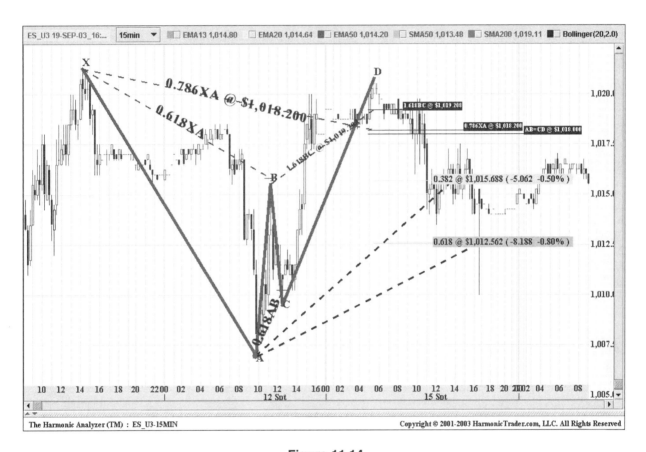

Figure 11.14

The contract reversed after testing all of the numbers in the PRZ, including the most significant number of the pattern, the AB=CD completion point at the 1018 level. The 0.786 XA retracement and the 1.618 BC projection just under the 1020 level complemented this harmonic resistance nicely.

I outlined this harmonic support in my pre-market Mini-Room Advisory post on HarmonicTrader.com on September 15, 2003.

"I would look for an early short position in this 1018 area."

(To review the actual recommendation, please go to http://www.HarmonicTrader.com/members/harmonic/home/ miniroom091503.htm.)

Figure 11.15

The chart in Figure 11.15 of price action in the PRZ shows an ideal reversal after a complete test the harmonic resistance. The ES stalled briefly following the initial test and declined sharply soon after violating the lower range of the PRZ.

The interesting aspect of this reversal was the time consideration at the pattern's completion. The chart in Figure 11.16 shows the spread of Fibonacci time calculations, as measured from the mid-point (B) and projected to the completion of the pattern. Initially, the CD leg of the Gartley pattern completed at the minimum 0.382 time projection. Although the initial test occurred at this minimum time constraint, the price action required more time to consolidate before the ultimate reversal. Although the ES already reversed sharply by the time the equivalent (1.0) time calculation was reached, the 0.382 time objective was an effective minimum time filter to validate the pattern's completion.

Figure 11.16

It is important to remember that the time requirement for a pattern's completion is not as important as the price objective. The key is to execute in the PRZ, as long as the minimum 0.382 time objective has been reached.

As the ES reversed, the IPO for this trade was set at the 0.382 retracement at 1015.68, as measured from the pattern. The ES exceeded this target, maintaining a steady downtrend throughout the day. Despite the impressive decline through the 38.2% IPO early in the session, the ES stalled for the rest of the day until the after-market (see Figure 11.17).

Figure 11.17

In this situation, the trade could have been covered after the 0.382 IPO was tested. Although the ES sank nominally lower later in the day, the lack of downside continuation in these situations should signal a warning that the reversal may not trade much past the IPO. The ES possessed a nice downtrend after the reversal was complete. The price action dropped sharply at the open and continued lower to the 0.382 IPO until midday (see Figure 11.18). The trend line and the 0.382 trailer were not broken until the overnight session the following day.

Figure 11.18

Although the sharp sell-off toward the end of the day traded down to the 0.618 profit target, the stalling action at the 0.382 I.P.O. triggered the short position to be covered in the1015 area. The violation of the trend line and the 38.2% retracement were distinct indications that this Bearish Gartley was likely to yield only a small profit. Despite the lackluster reversal, this trade in the ES exemplifies the entire Harmonic Trading process. A clear pattern was defined, the trade was executed in the PRZ, and the Harmonic Trade Management rules effectively guided the decision to cover the short position at a profit.

Furthermore, it is important to understand that harmonic patterns are not "end-all-be-all" price structures. I believe a common misconception is that harmonic patterns signal monster reversal every time. This is just not the case. In fact, this example of the ES is probably more common for most harmonic setups than the "home-run scenario." Especially with intra-day patterns, it is important to aggressively take partial profits at the IPO targets and apply the trade management rules strictly.

Dow Jones Industrial Diamonds (DIA): 30-Minute

The Dow Jones Industrial Diamonds formed this intra-day Bearish Butterfly on a 30-minute chart (see Figure 11.19). The setup possessed a convergence of numbers that defined the 96 level as critical short-term resistance. The Diamonds reversed exactly at the most significant number at the pattern's completion point—the 1.27 XA projection at 96.07. The AB=CD and the 2.24 BC projection complemented this harmonic resistance in the 96 area.

Figure 11.19

This chart in Figure 11.20 of price action in the PRZ shows an ideal reversal after a complete test of this harmonic resistance. The Diamonds quickly reversed from this zone and declined sharply following the completion of the pattern.

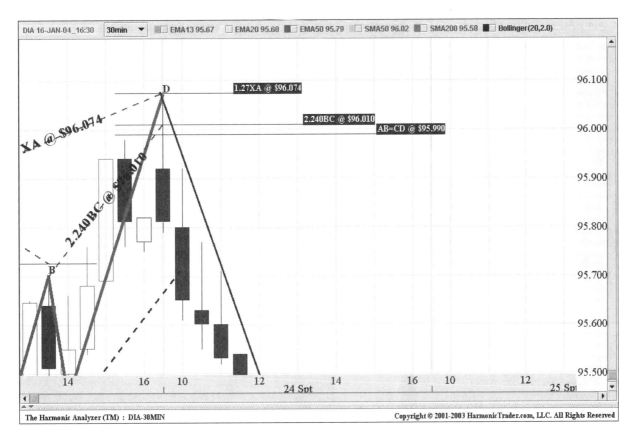

Figure 11.20

Figure 11.21 shows the spread of Fibonacci time calculations, as measured from the mid-point (B) and projected to the completion of the pattern. The CD leg rallied sharply into this PRZ but reversed exactly at the equivalent (1.0) time calculation. Perfect! Not only did the 1.0 time calculation result in the exact reversal point, but the PRZ defined the precise resistance level for the trade. Quite simply, it does not get any more ideal within the Harmonic Trading approach than this!

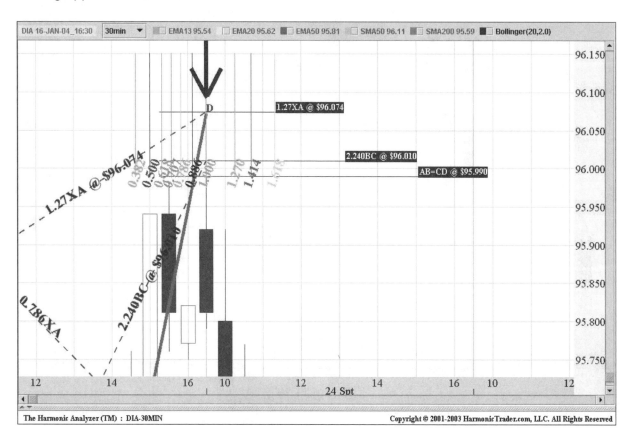

Figure 11.21

The Diamonds reversed sharply from this harmonic resistance and continued convincingly lower. The first downside target, the 0.382 IPO at 95.70 was easily taken out, as the reversal established a decisive downtrend from the pattern's high point. The next target at the 0.618 was quickly reached, as the Diamonds declined rapidly through this next target area. In fact, after the Diamonds hit the 0.618 target, the selling intensified, as the price action quickly tested the 0.886 and broke down past the pattern low.

The strong bearish continuation was particularly evidenced by the consistent formation of lower lows and lower highs formed by each price bar. In addition, throughout the day of the reversal, the Diamonds failed to break above any of the prior 30-minute highs.

After the pattern was complete, a steady sell-off ensued. This situation exemplifies the "home-run" reversal. The price action reversed exactly from the PRZ and possessed a magnificent bearish continuation. Each profit objective was clearly violated—even beyond the 1.618 extension of the pattern (see Figure 11.22). After the IPO targets at the 0.382 and the 0.618 had been exceeded, the most important consideration in the trade management of the position was the trend line from the reversal.

Figure 11.22

In this situation, the Diamonds formed a distinct downtrend that was eventually violated several days after the reversal was complete. The final trigger to cover the short occurred when the Diamonds took out the 0.382 trailing stop at 94.25.

It is important to note that not all valid harmonic patterns yield such a reversal. However, the Harmonic Trading Trade Management System is designed to allow enough "breathing room" for these reversals to assert themselves. In this case, the exact reversal and strong bearish continuation were the critical elements that identified this price action as a significant move (see Figure 11.23).

Figure 11.23

Partial Trade Management

As I mentioned previously, depending upon your trading preference, it can be advantageous to divide each position into two (or sometimes three) portions, securing partial profits at each target level while holding a portion of the original position for a larger move. I believe that this strategy is quite effective, especially when price action is volatile. One suggestion in this strategy is to place limit orders to cover a predetermined amount of the entire position exactly at the 0.382 and 0.618 IPO targets.

For simplicity's sake, I demonstrate the Harmonic Trade Management System with only a two-unit strategy. I typically secure a portion of the position when I get a trend line or 0.382 trailer violation, and cover the remainder at a more significant price objective depending upon the continuation of the reversal trend. I believe all traders have their own preference regarding this approach, and I leave it up to you to consider the best method for securing profits. However, I believe it is most advantageous to manage profitable trades in a multi-position manner.

Trade Management Tips

Identifying harmonic patterns is not a difficult skill to master. After studying the various patterns and applying the Fibonacci ratios, the trade as defined by the pattern completion point is usually quite clear. However, each position must be must be handled properly to maximize profits and minimize losses. Although two harmonic trades may possess the same patterns with identical Fibonacci ratios, their outcomes can be completely different. Therefore, there are some simple guidelines to follow during the management stage of a trade after it has been executed:

- **Be prepared for anything.** Although the clearest setups can indicate excellent trading opportunities, it does not relieve the responsibility of monitoring the trade and assuming everything will automatically work out. Therefore, it is critical to monitor price action closely.
- **Follow the trade management rules (execute in the PRZ).** The trade management rules are based upon years of harmonic research. Although they serve more as general guidelines, these strategies seek to optimize decisions in the trade management process by reducing relative risk while maximizing profit opportunities.
- **Respect the price bars at the harmonic levels.** The most critical information in a harmonic setup is derived from the price action at the convergence of numbers at a pattern's completion point. It is essential to closely examine how price action is responding when it hits a harmonic area. The nature of price action in well-defined pattern completion zones typically will indicate the overall validity of a setup. However, price action that fails to reverse in this area indicates that the predominant trend is quite strong.
- **Look for continuation.** After price action has reversed from a pattern's completion point, it should clearly continue in that direction. Price action that merely stalls or fails to move convincingly in the reversal trend usually indicates a potential failure.

- **Losses are a part of the business.** Although a majority of harmonic setups provide some degree of tradable reactions on the initial test of distinct pattern completions, a percentage of trades will fail. It is just a fact of the business of trading. The key is to cut the losses to a minimum and move on to the next trade. Trade executions will improve as experience develops the ability to quickly read the early signs of a reversal. Recognizing such failures, and reacting quickly to violated trade setups, preserves capital and prevents small losses from turning intro disastrous draw downs!
- **If in doubt, get out!** If you don't feel right about a trade or a position, close it out or don't take the trade. It is much safer to miss out on an opportunity than it is to anguish over a situation that is not inherently correct.

Trade management strategies of harmonic patterns require discipline and patience. Although this system attempts to maximize potential reversals, actual trade situations can involve many external factors that can influence the decision-making process. These rules are effective in allowing the market to offer the necessary price signals to validate reversals. Although there is room for discretion within this trade management system, these guidelines offer effective methods for handling trades and deciphering price action to maximize profits and minimize losses after a trade has been executed.

Chapter 12

Pattern Violations

When distinct harmonic patterns form, the anticipation of a valid reversal can frequently create a biased perspective of the assessment of the opportunity. For example, a perfect Bearish Bat could indicate a great selling opportunity. However, strong price action can blow out distinct patterns like these and trigger a continuation of the predominant trend. As the section "Warning Signs in the Potential Reversal Zone (PRZ)" in Chapter 10 illustrated, these situations frequently provide clear indication regarding the potential failure of a pattern. When this happens, there are defined strategies that can capitalize on the continuation of the predominant trend. The key to profiting from these situations is to utilize a strict trade management strategy with tight stop loss limits. After the pattern has been violated, the focus of any reversal pattern trade should examine the price action beyond the PRZ.

When trading a failed pattern setup, the trade management rules are more important, as this strategy leaves little room for anything other than the sharp continuation of the predominant trend beyond the violated PRZ. In addition, the reversal play can be tricky and frustrating, as frequent stop-outs can occur before the price continues in the predominant trend. Despite the potentially volatile price action associated with a failed pattern, these situations—when identified correctly—do offer excellent trading opportunities.

As I discussed previously, harmonic patterns define critical price levels within the predominant trend. Although patterns can accurately identify such pivot points, it is common for the predominant trend to eventually violate these defined price levels. These situations often provide ample opportunity to assess the validity of a particular pattern and offer specific price action signals that direct trading decisions.

The idea of trading a failed pattern bases its logic in the predominance of the existing trend. Since price bar warning signs frequently indicate potentially flawed harmonic patterns, they conversely can signal another opportunity of trading with the trend. Because pattern failures are a sign of an overwhelming predominant trend, these technical events can serve as important continuation signals. Instead of getting locked into the anticipation of a reversal at the completion of the pattern, this strategy takes more of a neutral approach. Trading executions are not limited to executing simple pattern completions. Moreover, strategies that take advantage of pattern failures capitalize on both types of signals that are generated from the price action in the Potential Reversal Zone. Regardless of the eventual result, the most important concept is that the completion of distinct harmonic patterns defines critical technical areas of support and resistance.

Reversing Failed Pattern Tips

- **The entire PRZ must be tested with initial reaction complete.** A continuation of the predominant trend usually occurs after the price action has tested the entire range of harmonic numbers in the PRZ. Although the extent of this nominal reaction varies, the price action usually does not retrace beyond the limits of the harmonic zone. Essentially, the initial test yields only a minor consolidation before resuming in the predominant trend to exceed the PRZ.
- **Respect the Terminal Price Bar.** The Terminal Price Bar—the initial price bar that tests the entire PRZ—establishes the defining limit for the violation of the PRZ. Furthermore, the Terminal Price Bar defines the reversal entry with respect to the failed PRZ.
- **Precise Stop Loss Limits.** All stop loss limits must be defined well in advance, and they usually are based upon the range of the prior PRZ and the extreme of the Terminal Price Bar.

After a pattern violation has been triggered, the reversal trade is usually executed one or two bars beyond the Terminal Price Bar. Typically, the violation should be a clear signal that confirms the continuation of the predominant trend. Beyond this point, the price action should convincingly trade in the direction of that trend. As the price action continues beyond the violated PRZ and the Terminal Price Bar, the stop loss in the trade management of the position is continually adjusted. In fact, after confirming the violation, the stop loss is usually determined by the prior price bar(s) beyond the Terminal Price Bar.

Reversing a Failed Bullish Pattern

In a failed bullish setup, the price action typically will experience some initial reaction to the completion of the pattern but quickly roll over violating the Terminal Price Bar (see Figure 12.1). It is common for the setup to experience sharp price action on the initial test of the PRZ. The critical element in a failed bullish pattern is a quick trend line violation of the first reaction. This is especially evident when a reversal experiences an impulse reaction in one or two price bars, only to immediately roll over and fail to continue to the upside. Although this requires some skilled interpretation to ascertain impending failures, such factors as a violation of a prior price bar low or breakdown of a short-term trend line of the reversal frequently signal trouble.

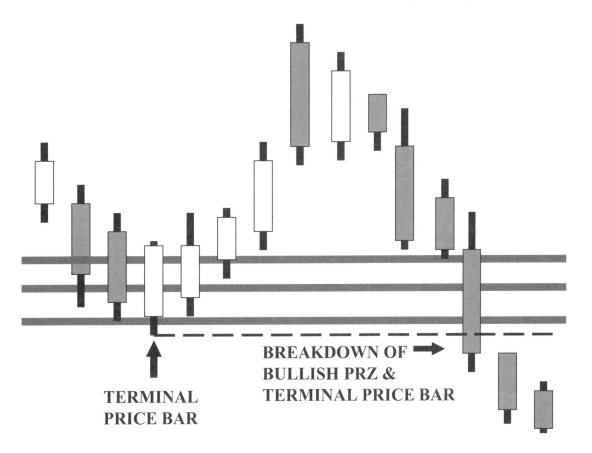

Figure 12.1

Another important element of a failed bullish pattern is the violation of the Terminal Price Bar. Ideally, the violation of the Terminal Price Bar and prior PRZ should close below the zone. Although this may appear as a "textbook" breakdown from a standard Technical Analysis perspective, such a violation of a prior harmonic zone is particularly important as clear confirmation of the pattern failure. In these situations, they can be considered a "harmonic breakdown."

Dow Jones Industrial Average ($INDU): Weekly

The Dow Jones Industrial Average exemplifies the ideal situation of a failed pattern. The index formed this Bullish Crab in Figure 12.2 and yielded a brief reversal for a few weeks from the Potential Reversal Zone (PRZ). Although the price action stabilized, the reversal fizzled. After a nominal rally that barely exceeded the top range of the PRZ, the index rolled over and declined sharply under the 10,700 level. Despite a perfect reversal from the 1.618 XA leg of the Crab, the reversal moved sideways after the initial pop. The lackluster bullish continuation signaled an impending failure long before the price action rolled over and sank decidedly lower in the direction of the predominant trend.

Figure 12.2

The first sign of trouble was the failure of the index to continue to the upside following the second week after the reversal. On the fourth week, the price action topped out and rolled over to retest the entire PRZ. Although the Terminal Price Bar was not yet violated at this point, the retest of the entire range of harmonic support should have raised a red flag in this situation.

The real signal of trouble was triggered on the violation of the PRZ of the second retest. Any long position executed at the initial completion of the Bullish Crab should have moved the stop loss limit to break even at a minimum. The chart in Figure 12.3 of the price action in the PRZ clearly shows the brief bounce and rollover that occurred.

Figure 12.3

The violation of this pattern led to a severe downside continuation in the 2009 bear market and it was a clear sign of the strength of the predominant downtrend. The weekly Bullish Crab was valid for a brief time, as the index temporarily found support at the initial completion of the pattern. The following few weeks followed a common scenario of many invalid setups, where a pattern yields only a short-term reversal, only to roll over shortly thereafter. The violation of the Terminal Price Bar in the PRZ on the second retest eventually triggered a deeper correction with a sharp (yet ideal) bearish continuation.

This chart example of the Industrials manifests a common aspect of many harmonic pattern trades and exemplifies the importance of executing on the initial test of a pattern's completion. Price action will frequently provide a short-term tradable reaction from the initial test of the PRZ. Furthermore, the nature of price action within the first few price bars after the entire range of harmonic numbers has been tested is the most critical aspect of the validation of a potential pattern. Although the index rolled over after a brief bounce, the initial reaction still provided a nice profit in the short-term. However, the index's failure to continue to the upside provided the necessary signals to exit the trade while protecting the small profit.

As I have mentioned previously, it is important to understand that harmonic patterns are not "end-all-be-all" price structures. I believe a common misconception is that harmonic patterns signal a monster reversal every time. This is just not the case. In fact, the example of the Dow Industrial Average is probably more common for most harmonic set-ups than the "home-run scenario." That is, distinct harmonic patterns offer a tradable reaction on their initial completion. For these reasons, Harmonic Trading techniques require an active trade management approach to fully maximize these common short-term reactive reversals. Although a longer-term perspective can be applied to utilize Harmonic Trading techniques from a weekly or monthly timeframe, the concept of specific profit targets and aggressive trade management is required to capitalize on these opportunities.

Another important consideration of this strategy is the discipline required to effectively manage these trades. The defined trade management parameters instill greater confidence and responsibility for every position. In the same manner that specific elements are required to identify harmonic price patterns, the price action in valid reversals must behave in a particular fashion, exhibiting the commonalities of a change in trend. In the Dow case, the initial bounce offered evidence of a reversal at hand. However, the clear failure to continue to the upside shortly after the reversal signaled the impending rollover.

If the position was going to be flipped, where the long position was covered and a new short position was entered, the second test of the Potential Reversal Zone (PRZ) was the critical area. As the previous scenario demonstrated, the initial long position would have been exited in the Profit Protection Zone (PPZ), somewhere close to the break down at 11,200 and certainly before a complete retest of the original entry point. Although this rollover was quite evident within weeks after the initial PRZ test, the pattern was not considered a failure until the violation of the Terminal Price Bar at the 10,700 level. Any short position that was seeking to capitalize on this failure should have been entered on this violation. Again, in these situations, the price action should clearly continue in the predominant trend, quickly declining below the prior PRZ.

As a failed pattern trade, the short executed following the violation of the harmonic support should have utilized a tight stop loss limit and be placed just above the prior week's high. In this case, the stop loss would be executed above the 11,300 level, which was the top range of the prior PRZ. As the failed pattern reversal trade continued to work out, the stop loss limit should have been adjusted accordingly, maintaining an active approach throughout the management of the position. In the Dow case, a simple 1-bar stop loss would have been more than adequate.

IBM
(IBM): Weekly

This example of IBM shows a distinct Bullish Butterfly that was violated after a brief bounce from the initial test of the Potential Reversal Zone (see Figure 12.4). It is important to note that the alignment of Fibonacci numbers in the pattern structure were ideal, as the 1.27 XA and 1.618 BC projections converged in the same area as the AB=CD completion point just under $80 a share.

Figure 12.4

The chart in Figure 12.5 of the price action on the PRZ clearly shows the brief bounce and rollover that occurred. In this example as well as the IBM chart, the first sign of trouble was the failure of the stock to continue to the upside following the second week after the reversal.

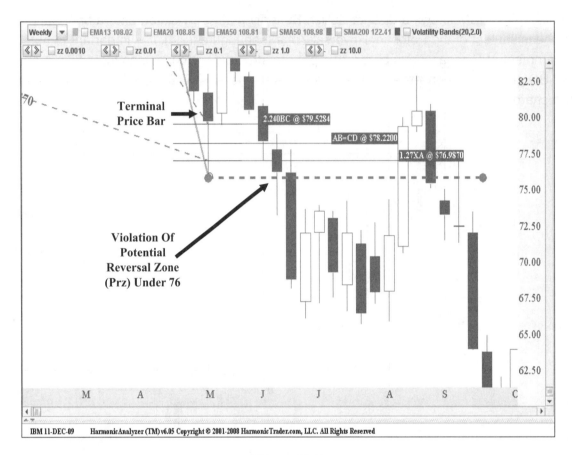

Figure 12.5

After a sharp move to the $85 level, IBM stalled. By the fifth week, the stock rolled over, retesting the entire PRZ. Although the Terminal Price Bar was not yet violated until the following week, the retest of the entire range of harmonic support should have raised a red flag.

As this example of IBM demonstrates, the lack of continuation following a reversal is frequently an early indication of a potential pattern failure. Although such failures are not immediately discernable in every situation, this case of IBM exemplifies the "window of time" available within the early stages of most reversals that offer a few price bars to signal the potential direction of the future price action. Ideally, pattern reversals should hit the entire PRZ on the initial test, reverse close to this range of harmonic numbers, and possess a strong continuation of the new trend. For IBM, one bullish price bar off the PRZ does not establish a new trend. Figure 12.5 shows the price action in the Potential Reversal Zone with the Terminal Price Bar clearly labeled.

Despite this rollover, the initial bounce yielded a nice short-term profit, as the stock bounced 9 points before rolling over. At a minimum, the Bullish Butterfly offered a great short-term opportunity. But, this is another example of a clear harmonic pattern yielding only a brief move that required an aggressive trade management approach to protect the initial profit and handle the position effectively. If anything, the rollover and violation of the bullish pattern signaled a continuation of the predominant bearish trend.

If the position was going to be flipped, where the long position was covered and a new short position was entered, the second test of the PRZ was the critical area. As this situation illustrates, the initial long position would have been exited in the PPZ, somewhere between the breakdown at $80 and the entry point under $77. Although this rollover was evident within weeks after the initial reversal, the pattern was not considered a failure until the violation of the Terminal Price Bar at the $76 level. Any short position that was seeking to capitalize on this failure should have been entered on this violation.

The solid downtrend line illustrated on the chart exemplifies the effectiveness of this constraint in well-defined breakdowns. The price action was clearly sliding in an area that was supposed to yield a reversal, as defined by the Bullish Butterfly. Despite the ideal alignment of numbers, the predominant bearish trend line contained the price action, pushing the stock lower after a brief reversal off the initial completion of the pattern.

This is another example of a sharp downside continuation following the violation of the Terminal Price Bar serving as an important continuation trigger. These situations are common, as the violation of distinct harmonic zones frequently encounter sharp continuations of the predominant trend.

Again, this is another scenario where it is important to understand that harmonic patterns are not "end-all-be-all" price structures. The IBM example demonstrates the type of short-term reversals that frequently materialize after the completion of a distinct harmonic setup. Although not every pattern will yield a "home-run," most reversals will yield small reactions at a minimum, offering profitable short-term trading opportunities.

Another important aspect of the IBM example is the ability of distinct patterns like this sharp Bullish Butterfly in IBM to serve as a "**signpost of future action**." I initially discussed this in *The Harmonic Trader*, and I have expounded on the concept throughout this book. Patterns should represent a price structure signal that must be assessed from a pragmatic viewpoint. Essentially, it comes down to these two rules:

1. **All patterns are not the same.**
2. **All reversals are not the same.**

Therefore, it is important to not assume that a distinct pattern will always yield a "home-run" reversal. Rather, it is critical to be prepared to utilize the signals that are offered by the market's price action in these harmonic zones to guide trading decisions.

Harmonic Trading techniques offer excellent opportunities but require an active trade management approach to fully maximize these common short-term reactive reversals. Although a longer-term perspective can be applied to utilize Harmonic Trading techniques to analyze weekly or monthly time frames, the concept of specific profit targets and aggressive trade management are still required to capitalize on most harmonic opportunities.

Reversing a Failed Bearish Pattern

In a failed bearish setup, illustrated in Figure 12.6, the price action typically will experience some initial reaction to the completion of the pattern but quickly turn back up to retest the Potential Reversal Zone (PRZ), eventually violating the Terminal Price Bar. I like to refer to these situations as "harmonic breakouts," where price action rallies above distinct harmonic zones of well-defined patterns.

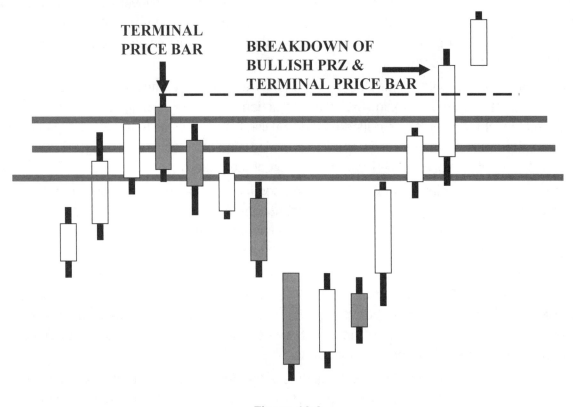

Figure 12.6

Harmonic breakouts above distinct bearish PRZs typically possess extreme price bars and convincing bullish continuation. These breakouts are especially significant in retracement patterns like the Bat and the Gartley, and can serve as excellent entry to signals to follow the predominant trend.

Intel
(INTC): 60-Minute

This chart of a failed Bullish AB=CD pattern in Intel is an ideal example that yielded a brief reversal from the Potential Reversal Zone (PRZ), only to continue sharply higher in the direction of the predominant trend (see Figure 12.7).

Figure 12.7

Briefly after the stock stalled at the pattern's completion, the Terminal Price Bar and the PRZ were violated convincingly. Illustrated on the chart in Figure 12.8 of the price action in the PRZ, Intel rallied sharply above the initial test of the AB=CD completion by gapping up on the open of the following day's trading.

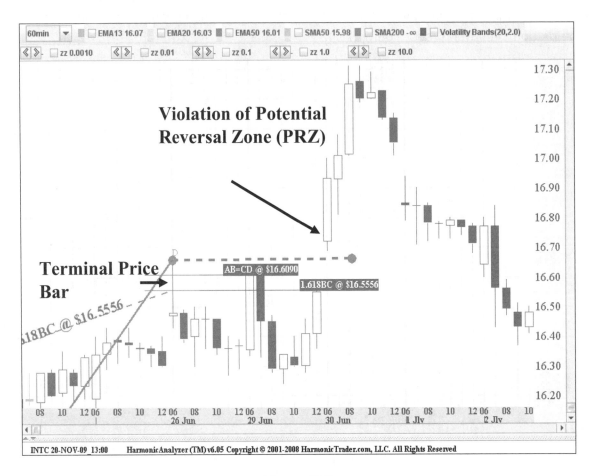

Figure 12.8

Such breakouts above defined harmonic patterns like this setup frequently can act as a trigger to reverse the initial trade idea and follow the predominant trend. After Intel broke out above the Terminal Price Bar, the stock steadily climbed, possessing a nice bullish continuation with a distinct trend line support that defined the rally.

These situations are common, and this example demonstrates the ability of blown-out patterns to act as signposts of future action. In this case, the violated AB=CD clearly indicated the strength of the rally in the stock. It is important to note that reversing a bearish setup must occur after the violation of the Terminal Price Bar, as the sharp continuation anticipated in these setups usually does not occur until this is exceeded. In this chart of Intel, the stock did not significantly rally until the Terminal Price Bar was violated above $16.65. Again, it is important to maintain a tight stop loss limit when attempting to play the continuation of the predominant trend, as the price action should continue decidedly above the prior PRZ.

Amazon.com (AMZN): Weekly

Amazon formed a distinct Bearish Butterfly with an ideal alignment of Fibonacci ratios to validate the structure (see Figure 12.9). The pattern defined a shorting opportunity in an approximate 1-point range between 25.75–26.95. Despite the clear pattern, the stock rallied sharply on the week it tested the PRZ. After the action stalled for several weeks, the stock rocketed above the Terminal Price Bar and the prior bearish PRZ.

Figure 12.9

The violation of the bearish pattern signaled a strong continuation of the predominant bullish trend (see Figure 12.10). If the position was going to be flipped, where the short position was covered and a new long position was entered, the violation of the Terminal Price Bar above the $28 level was the determining area.

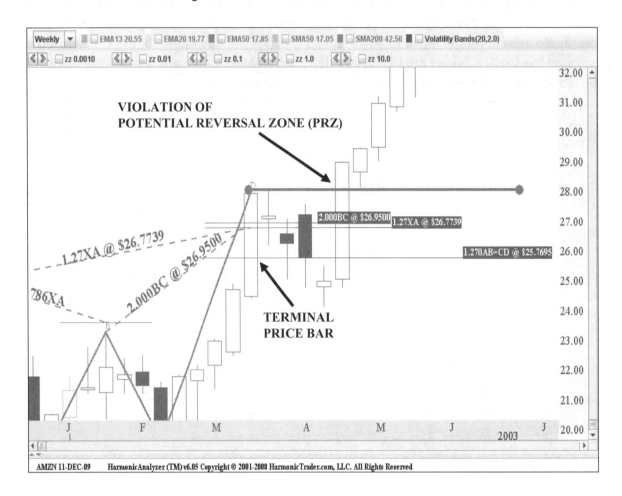

Figure 12.10

This is another example of a decisive upside continuation following the violation of the Terminal Price Bar. These situations are common, as the violation of distinct harmonic zones frequently triggers sharp continuations of the predominant trend. In this case, Amazon rallied convincingly in the weeks following the Terminal Price Bar breakout, as the stock continued to rally into higher territory while holding the prior weeks' lows.

Prior Harmonic Support and Resistance

Static support and resistance levels have been a foundation of Technical Analysis for decades. Price action tends to trade in zones of support and resistance. When support is violated, that price level becomes future resistance. When resistance is violated, that price level becomes future support.

Although this is a simple concept to grasp, when applied to the PRZ of harmonic patterns, this concept can identify critical price levels that otherwise might be overlooked. After clear harmonic patterns are violated, the price action usually continues in the predominant trend for some time. However, it is common for price action to retest these harmonic levels, as prior patterns frequently mark critical points within an overall trend.

Prior Harmonic Support as Resistance

When the Potential Reversal Zone (PRZ) of a bullish pattern is blown out or violated, the prior harmonic support commonly acts as future resistance when the price action retests this level.

NASDAQ 100 Continuous Mini-Contract (NQ_#F): 15-Minute

This chart of the NASDAQ 100 Continuous Mini-contract illustrates the concept of prior harmonic support acting as resistance. On this 15-minute chart, the NQ clearly violated the intra-day Bullish Bat early in the session (see Figure 12.11). The pattern defined the area just in the area of 1780 as critical short-term harmonic support. However, the contract was sliding in the pre-market and continued sharply lower after the open. Despite the breakdown, the NQ rallied back to retest this prior support later in the day.

Figure 12.11

The structural failure of the prior harmonic support zone clearly was a key intra-day level. The ability of pattern completion points to define important technical levels is a unique phenomenon within the Harmonic Trading approach. The ability to interpret these signals increases with experience, but it is important to respect the information that such pattern failures provide.

Semiconductor Holder's Trust (SMH): 10-Minute

The Semiconductor Holder's Trust (SMH) blew out this Deep Bearish Crab on the 10-minute chart (see Figure 12.12). After gapping well above the PRZ on the open, the SMH retraced a good portion of the initial pop. The price action refilled the upside gap and bounced in the area where prior *harmonic* resistance acted as clear support. The intra-day Bearish Butterfly was blown out after gapping past the PRZ on the open of the trading, the day it tested these numbers.

Figure 12.12

After completely violating the prior bearish setup, the SMH retraced some of the rally, finding support in an area of prior harmonic resistance. It is important to note that the SMH filled the intra-day gap in the same area as the prior resistance. These situations are common and frequently define nice short-term trading opportunities.

Although these prior PRZs should be utilized with other current patterns to define trading opportunities, this phenomenon within the realm of Harmonic Trading techniques is extremely effective. These situations are most commonly found when a pattern has been clearly violated. Despite these failed pattern setups, prior PRZs can provide a great deal of information regarding the potential direction of future price action that might otherwise be overlooked.

The chart in Figure 12.13 of price action in the violated PRZ exemplifies this phenomenon, as prior harmonic support became considerable short-term resistance.

Figure 12.13

Pattern Violation Conclusion

The concept of prior blown-out PRZs acting as an opposite technical level is founded in the principle that harmonic patterns are primarily a "signpost of future action." I initially discussed this in *The Harmonic Trader*. Essentially, the critical information is revealed by the price action in the Potential Reversal Zone (PRZ). Although valid patterns are quite accurate and identify excellent trading opportunities, there are many cases where the predominant trend overwhelms the anticipated completion of a pattern. Despite the failed reversal, the distinct price action at the completion of a pattern frequently possesses extraordinary behavior that acts as a clear signal for the continuation of the predominant trend.

Conclusion

The purpose of *Harmonic Trading: Volume One* is to clarify and define the numerous price structures that comprise the foundation of the Harmonic Trading methodology. I believe the specification of price structures within the realm of Harmonic Trading is among the most advanced Fibonacci analysis utilized in Technical Analysis. It is in this precise specification that Harmonic Trading possesses its greatest advantages, yielding an accurate and effective means of identifying potential trading opportunities.

Although Harmonic Trading techniques possess a powerful array of pattern identification methods, the ultimate success and profitability of this approach requires an effective and aggressive trade management strategy. As the numerous chart examples demonstrated, most pattern completions yield sizeable but temporary price moves that require an active trade management strategy to maximize returns. Although Harmonic Trading techniques are extremely effective in long-term and general market analysis, the same trade management concepts should be utilized short-term situations to determine the critical signals that indicate the potential future price action.

Harmonic Trading: Volume One is a comprehensive foundation for most of the Harmonic Trading techniques. A great deal of material covered in *The Harmonic Trader*—such as the Three Drives pattern, prior gaps, and the importance of Volume—is not in this material. However, I believe this book possesses a thorough methodology from pattern identification to trade execution through the entire trade management process.

Already in the development stages, *Harmonic Trading: Volume Two* will build upon this comprehensive foundation, adding many advanced techniques to all stages of the trading process. In addition, I will be releasing two new harmonic patterns in *Volume Two*. I look forward to continuing my research in the realm of Harmonic Trading and sharing these ideas in future material.

The most important concept to understand from this material is that Harmonic Trading is different from all other forms of Technical Analysis and Fibonacci approaches to the financial markets. Unprecedented discoveries such as the Bat pattern, the Alternate AB=CD structures, the 0.886 retracement, the Harmonic Trade Management System, and other techniques offer advantages that no other technical approach offers. Simply stated, "This is not just another Fibonacci methodology, this is Harmonic Trading."

Best Regards,
Scott M. Carney

Bibliography

Carney, Scott M. *The Harmonic Trader*. Nevada: HarmonicTrader.com, LLC, 1999.

Cootner, Paul H. *The Random Character of Stock Market Prices*. Massachusetts: MIT Press, 1964.

Gann W. D. *How to Make Profits in Commodities*. New York: New York Institute of Finance, 1942.

Gann W. D. *Tunnel Thru the Air*. Pomeroy, WA: Lambert-Gann Publishing, 1927.

Gartley, H. M. *Profits in the Stock Market*. Pomeroy, WA: Lambert-Gann Publishing, 1935.

Hurst, J. M. *J. M. Hurst Cycles Course*. Greenville, SC: Traders Press, 1970.

Hurst, J. M. *The Profit Magic of Stock Transaction Timing*. Greenville, SC: Traders Press, 1970.

Kane, Jim. *Advanced Fibonacci Trading Concepts*. Tucson, AZ: KaneTrading.com, 2003.

Prechter, Robert. *Elliott Wave Principle*. Gainesville, GA: New Classics Library, 1978.

Index

C